GOD *at* EVENTIDE

A Companion-Volume
to
GOD CALLING
by
Two Listeners

EDITED BY A. J. RUSSELL

A BARBOUR BOOK

In response to many requests for a companion-volume to *God Calling*, this book was born.

Though like *God Calling*, it makes no claim to throw new light on old truths, it is sent out with the prayer that it will be the means for showing readers more clearly what Christ may become to those who seek to know Him and to live with Him.

ISBN 1-55748-312-4

Published by BARBOUR AND COMPANY, INC.
P.O. Box 719
Uhrichsville, OH 44683

Printed in the United States of America

JANUARY

All Is Ready   January 1

WRITE for all things are now ready.

The world is waiting for My Message of Love, and Hope and Cheer. The very unrest of spirit is a sign. The turning from the husk of religion is a sign.

Man is no longer lulled by empty phrases and promises of a better life hereafter. He must *know* Me before he would wish to spend Eternity with Me. He must know Me here in the storm where he needs strength and rest.

He has been sleeping; now he has been shocked awake. Now he must find Me or fling defiance at Me or school himself into denial, or indifference.

Reason and argument avail nothing. Only by the lives of My followers can man be helped; only by seeing Mine unmoved, at peace, joyful, in a world of sorrow, disillusionment and mistrust.

Your denial to-day will not be "I know not the man." The world is indifferent as to whether you *profess* Me or not. No, it will be your failure to present Me in your life as I am—vital, sustaining, spirit-renewing, your All.

Your Resolutions   January 2

IT is in union with Me that you receive strength to carry out your good resolutions.

Contact with Me brings power for the work I wish you to do, that work for which I know you to be most suited and which you only can do, and do so well.

It is in contact with Me that you are endued with the Grace that I alone can give, enabling you to minister acceptably to those to whom I send you, and those whom I bring to you.

Even among the distractions and manifold interests of the world—live in My Presence, yet daily withdraw yourself to be *alone* with Me.

Mutual Need   January 3

Abide in Me and I in you.

THIS year dwell much upon this stupendous Truth. *You* need to abide in Me this year to share in the Spirit-life of the Universe, in its creative power and energy. Thus you are a part in God's whole.

But *I* must abide in you, for only so can I express My Love and Power and Truth through you interpreting them in deed, and look, and word.

In these words of Mine you have My two-fold nature.

The Strong Protector! so Strong to shield; and offering you, My guest, all provision you need.

And then you have Me in My Humility, one with you, your close Companion, dwelling in you, and dependent on you. Think on these things.

HERE in this evening hour I draw near to you—
and listen. Tell Me of the Peace you know in
Me; of the tender confidence in Me that has
brought Peace and Safety into your life.

To-morrow you will go back into the world
with My message of Eternal Life. Truths that you
are only just beginning fully to grasp, that are
bringing you Vision and Joy, you will pass to
others, that they may be saved the wasted years
that lie behind you. Turn to them as you would
to one following you along a dangerous road and
warn them against the pitfalls in their way.

Point out to them the beauties of the *The Way*,
the sunlit hills ahead, the sunset glories, the streams
and flowers of My peaceful glades.

Direct their attention from earth's allures or
mirages to Me, your Companion of The Way.
Tell them of your Joy in Me. That is your man-
date from High Heaven.

The Healing Hour January 5

As yet you can only dimly see what this evening-
time will mean for you.

For a while you shed earth's cares and frets,
and know the uplift of soul that comes through
planned Communion with Me.

You are renewed, and that renewing is your
safeguard from mental and spiritual disintegration.

In this brief time you taste, in contact with
Me, something of My Resurrection Life. It is the

glorified Christ you know, and to know Him is to partake too of His Risen Life.

Thus health, physical, mental and spiritual, comes to you and flows from you.

Land of Promise   January 6

IMAGINE the Hope of My Heart that day on the mountain-side when I told My followers that to no throne on earth I led them; old forms and negations that had meant so much in the past were to be swept away; motives and impulses were to be all-important.

By the thoughts of his heart was a man to be judged. Prayer was like a son appealing to a father. Love was to be the foundation, the Golden Rule. Tribal, even racial, distinctions were to be ignored and the claims of the whole great family of God were to be met.

To such heights as they had never before scaled I led them, up to Peak-truths they had thought unscalable.

What hopes I had of them as their wonder turned to Vision and they responded to My Message.

What hopes I have to-day of each of you My Followers as you catch sight of your Land of Promise ahead.

> *I am the True Light that cometh into the world, and men love darkness rather than Light, because their deeds are evil.*

TRULY not all men desire My Light. Not all men would welcome its clear shining.

Many shrink from its revelation, preferring the darkness that would hide their deeds, rather than the remorseless Light that would show the evil of which they are ashamed.

Pray for Light, rejoice to have it, welcome its revelation, and so, when in your lives it has done its searching, cleansing work, then bear it yourselves gladly, triumphantly, out into a world that needs so sorely the Light of the World.

I CALL upon you to make Me known—

> *By your unfailing trust in Me.*
>
> *By your joy, unrepressed by the difficulties of the way.*
>
> *By your tender concern for the weak and the wandering.*
>
> *By your acceptance of My Gift of Eternal Life.*
>
> *By your growth in Spiritual development, proof of that inner life, which alone can engender it.*

Make Me known, more and more, by your serenity, by unflinching adherence to Truth.

Make Me known by My Spirit within and

round you, your conduct and speech ever bearing witness to the Power and the Wonder of My Presence.

So shall all men know that you are My disciple, and that your claim is never for the recognition of the self—but for Me, the Christ-in-you.

A Love-Home January 9

HUSH earth's desires that you miss not My Footfall. It brings the strength of a warrior, and the eagerness of a Lover.

Let your heart thrill with the glad, "He comes." Forsake all thought but the thought of Me as I enter. Soul-rest and heart-comfort I bring. Forget all else.

Let Me lift the burden from your shoulders, My burden, borne for you. Here in quiet, we will rest, while you are reinvigorated.

Poor dwelling, you feel, for the King of Kings. Yet I see your Home of Love as Love has made it. I come from locked doors, where youth is trying to live without Me; where old age, ever refusing to answer My pleading and knocking, now hears Me no more, and sits silent and alone.

Comfort Me, My children. Make of your hearts a Love-Home for the Man of Sorrows, still so often despised and rejected of men. Yet I would turn their sorrow into joy.

How Self Dies

HUSH your spirit still more in My Presence. Self dies, not by human combat, not necessarily by supplicatory prayer, but by the consciousness of My Presence, and of My Spirit-values. Thus self shrivels into lifelessness, into nothingness.

It is so necessary to dwell with Me, to draw so close to Me in an understanding as complete as it is possible for man to realize.

Do you not see now the need for the training and discipline I have enjoined on you? They are vital in that they attune your being to the consciousness of My Mind and Purpose. When this Mind is in you that is in Me you are able to penetrate the outer courts of the Temple, and in the very Holy of Holies to grasp the meaning that lay behind all I said and did and was.

Sacrifice all for this. Your work has to be inspired. Where can you find inspiration but in My Presence?

YOUR Good News

"How beautiful upon the mountains are the feet of those who bring glad tidings . . . that publish Peace." When you are weary think that yours are the feet of those who bring glad tidings.

This will rob your steps of weariness, will give a Joy and a spring to your walk.

"Bringeth glad tidings. Publisheth Peace." What a joyful mission. One of gladness and Peace. Never forget this, and the Joy of your message and mission will radiate from you gladdening and transforming.

Bright Shadows January 12

He descended into Hell . . . He ascended into Heaven.

IT is good for man to know his Lord is ever with him through every danger, every change, every seeming chance. It is good to walk the dark waters with Me.

I did not make the darkness. It was no artist-design to create a darkness which should make My Light seem the greater radiance.

Wilfulness and sin have caused earth's shadows, but I am there to walk the dark places with you. So that even the darkest place may be illumined by the Light of the Sun of Righteousness.

Fight Evil Forces January 13

YOU are going to be a mighty force against evil because you will be ever-increasingly the agent of Divine Power. Think, when this is so, how could you for one moment imagine that evil could leave you alone? It is to the advantage of evil to thwart you.

Think how those who care for you in the Unseen watch to see you conquer in My strength for My Glory.

The great battles of your world are fought in the Unseen. Fight there your battles and win. More than conquerors through Him Who loves you.

Fight with the whole armour of God, ready prepared for you.

Victors through Me. Press on, Victory is in sight.

How Joy Comes   January 14

THE Joy that follows awareness of Guidance has ever been the upholding Joy of My followers.

It is the result of desiring My Will only, in every detail, and then the realization of the wonderful way I can act for you *when you leave the planning to Me*.

Truly all things, every detail in each day, do work together for good to those who love Me. My miracle-working power can become operative when there is no "kicking against the pricks," no thwarting of My Will.

Whether you walk here on earth, or are free from earth's limitations in My Heaven, it is Heaven to walk with Me. Man has sought to describe Heaven in terms of music and song. That is but his endeavour to express the ecstasy he knows on earth in Communion with Me, and to anticipate its magnified intensity in Heaven.

Where Danger Lies   January 15

I AM beside you—the eager Listener, so ready to hear your plea, so ready to say all that your heart needs.

Live more with Me apart, and so there will come an ever-increasing helpfulness to others.

Heart-poise, mental balance, spiritual strength, will be yours in ever more abundant measure. Never feel that you can help others unaided by Me, for therein lies danger.

Your self-importance is destructive of helpfulness, devitalising because *your* strength has such limitations. Mine is limitless.

Grow more dependent upon Me, yet more assured that you can do all things through Me.

The Foe Within   January 16

NEVER lose heart. Kill the proud self as you go on, for on that dead self you rise.

On ever with Me. Do not let earth's frets disturb you. Since you cannot follow Me and indulge self, at all costs turn self out directly its claims disturb; so only can you keep spiritual calm.

Not your circumstances but your *self* is the enemy. A man's foes are those of his own household.

Do others blame you falsely? I was reviled but I reviled not again.

Great Souls   January 17

I AM here. Realise My Presence. My love surrounds you; be filled with My Joy.

You are being truly guided though not until you are content to be led as little children do *you* really live fully in the Kingdom of Heaven.

Life with Me is of child-like simplicity. Simple souls are the great souls, for in simplicity there is majesty.

Joy of Meeting

So many think of prayer as petition only. It IS petition. "In everything by prayer and supplication let your requests be made known unto Me."

But prayer is also a glad turning to meet Me for the joy of the meeting, for the rapture of My Presence.

Prayer, too, is preparation for to-morrow's return to those who need you, those to whom My love goes out from you.

Comfort and Joy

I AM with you. I will help you. Through suffering to health, through sorrow to joy, through pain to ease, through night to day—you shall be led and comforted.

Without previous experience of dawn and day none could dream that the glorious dawn and fulness of day could follow the blackest night.

Regard this experience not as darkness but as dawn. The first faint glimmers of light are following the black night through which you have passed. The full day is not yet. But hail the DAWN with Me.

Now Is the Victory

I AM with you. I am delivering you. But look for deliverance not from circumstances alone, but deliverance from the self-ties that bind you to earth, and that hinder your entrance into that kingdom of service in which there is perfect freedom. All is well.

You shall rise to newness of Life. You cannot fail to rise as you free yourself from the toils and sins and failures that bind you to earth.

No past sin can enchain you. You look to Me and are saved. They are all forgiven. Conquer your faults with My Strength now, and nothing can prevent you from rising, nothing that is past.

Exceeding Great Reward   January 21

I am thy shield and thine exceeding great reward.

SHIELD from the storm of life. Shield from even the consequences of your own faults and failings. Shield from your weakness. Shield from worry. Shield from fear and sorrow. Shield from the world with its allure and temptations. Not only your shield, but your exceeding great reward.

Not the reward of perfection in your life, for that you could not win here. Not the reward of what you do, or of any merit in yourself. Only the result, or reward of your questing. The satisfaction of your hunger to find Me. Exceeding great reward.

Your reward is the same as that of the greatest saint who has ever lived. Given not as a trophy of victory, not as a recognition of virtue, but given because you are the seeker, and I, your Lord, am the Sought.

I Know All   January 22

I AM the sharer of the secrets of your life. How

rich in blessing each experience may be if shared with Me alone.

How often, by much speaking and self-indulgent sharing with others, a jewel or rare beauty may be robbed of its priceless worth to your soul. A bud of Joy and sweet perfume too rashly forced to premature bloom will lose its purity and fragrance.

Even the sharing of past sins and failures may mean self for the time in the foreground, or vitality, so needed for the present, lost. Dwell in the Secret Place of the Most High.

Fear No Evil   January 23

I AM the Lord of your life, Guardian of your inmost being, the Christ of God. Sheltered in My Hidden Place no harm can befall you. Pray to know this.

Let this Truth become a part of your very consciousness, that where I am no evil can be, and that therefore when you abide in Me and I in you no evil can touch you.

Spiritual Truths take sometimes many years to learn, sometimes they come in a flash of sudden revelation.

Have You?   January 24

I AM teaching you, but not always Spiritual Truths that gladden you.

Often, too often, there has to be the word of reproof as I tell you of commands of Mine not obeyed, of resolutions made when in contact with

Me that you have failed to keep, of work done for Me in no spirit of Love and Joy, of failure to obtain supply because your attitude (often not your heart) questioned My *unlimited* supply.

I teach no easy lesson.

I choose no flower-bordered path in which to walk with you, but take heart that I *do* walk with you as with Peter of old even when he denied Me.

He had seen his sin. He went out and wept bitterly.

My Compensations — January 25

I AM listening. Picture Me, your Lord. Not as one deaf to your entreaties, but rather as One straining with an intensity of Love to catch the first faint cry from one of His children.

Even in the case of those who love Me, how often do I listen in vain for the spontaneous words of Love?

Do not cry to Me only when cares press and you are weary. Speak to Me often. Share with Me all the little happenings, all the frets, all the little glad things.

These not only draw us more closely to each other, but they are to Me compensations for the neglect I suffer from My world.

The Healing Life — January 26

I AM your Lord, trust Me in all. Never doubt My keeping Power. Behold Me, the Lord of your life. Gain strength from Me.

Remember that Healing, Divine Healing, is not so much a question of praying on your part, and of granting on Mine, as of living with Me, thinking of Me, sharing My Life. That contact makes you whole. Go forward gladly, go forward unafraid.

Help for All   January 27

I HAVE not promised My Help to the virtuous only. To the sinner who turns to Me, to the saint who lives with Me, to both alike My miracle-working Power is manifested.

Help, temporal as well as spiritual, truly I bestow, not as a reward of goodness but as a fulfilment of My pledge made to all who believe in Me.

But when one turns to Me I at once plan the rescue craved. If that one hearing My plan, learning of My Purpose, should fail to do his appointed task in that plan, how can My healing of physical, spiritual or temporal disharmony be manifested?

Your Defender   January 28

I AM the Gift of God to man. Only so was it possible for man to know God the Father. Only so was it possible for man to know that he had ever an Advocate with God—the Sinless Christ.

There is always One Who understands your case, Whose appeal cannot fail to be heard. He has the right of Sonship. He has a right to plead for you.

If he can plead for offending man, undertaking full responsibility for him, what better Advocate could you have? He knows. He has seen the tears of sorrow, the heartache and temptation. He can plead as none other.

His own temptation was so real that, conqueror as He was, He can yet feel the tenderest pity for the vanquished. He knows how seeming fair evil can appear, and He can estimate the added burden of tainted blood, inherited weakness and sin.

He gave His only Begotten Son. This GREAT GIFT AM I, your Friend, your Companion. Leave all to Me, your Advocate, trained during My years on earth to plead, never for Myself, but for every one who rests his cause in My Hands.

Overcomers   January 29

STUDY the "Overcomeths" in the Revelation to My servant John, and you will see the tender intimacy with Me promised as a result of overcoming. To believe is not enough. To believe in Me does truly involve the possession of Eternal Life, but that is a trust to *use* as truly as the talent of My story.

It is not only a something to be *enjoyed*.

Eternal life is a refreshing, reforming, enriching, uprooting, ennobling Power to be *employed* to the full by those to whom I entrust it.

In this My servants so often fail, and so miss the wonder of Communion with Me. Guard this Truth.

More Love   January 30

I COME, a truly willing guest. Love always draws.

Remember that. Love is the magnetic Power of the Universe. God is LOVE, the Power that draws all men by various ways unto Himself.

Remember that your Love too, being of God, has the same magnetic Power. Love, and you will draw to you those whom you desire to help.

When you fail to do so, search your life. Love is deficient. More love is necessary.

The Evening Call   January 31

SOFTLY at even, comes the footfall of your Master. My day has been long and weary. Hearts that I have yearned over and longed for still withstand Me.

I see the aged, desolate without Me. I see the disappointment of men and women, who in Me would find heart-satisfaction which others cannot give them. I see youth crowding Me out of its work-filled, pleasure-filled days. And yet I wait. I knock, I plead, I call, unheard, unheeded, unwanted.

As I was the link between the Father and man, so now must My followers be the links between man and Me.

Human Love, material aid, human understanding and friendship must bind those for whom I yearn.

Channels through which My help can flow to man truly you must be, but also the means through which man finds his groping way to Me.

EVENING AND MORNING

O let me hear Thee speaking
   In accents clear and still,
Above the storms of passion,
   The murmurs of self-will.

O speak to reassure me,
   To hasten, or control;
O speak, and make me listen,
   Thou Guardian of my soul!

FEBRUARY

All Loves Excelling

Softly I approach. Gently My Spirit speaks to your heart.

The mystery of man's communion with Me lies in the beauty and wonder of its aloneness. For the moment the world seems not to exist. Its noise and traffic seem hushed.

There is indeed wonder in that stillness. A faint glimpse is seen in the sudden realization of Love between two human beings. Surprise and wonder . . . the world is for them alone . . . no claim other than their love.

What wonder in the heart of man when he realizes the beauty, tenderness and closeness of Communion with Me!

My Wages

If the world understands you, then you are speaking its language, actuated by its motives, living its life according to its standards. Will you have this?

Remember I said very clearly, "Ye cannot serve God and mammon." If you serve God, then, for your work, you should surely look to God for reward.

So many of My servants serve Me, and yet expect to receive the gratitude and praise, or at least the acknowledgement of the world. Why? You are not doing the work of the world. Why expect its pay?

Ambassadors All   February 3

IF you love Me and long to serve others by showing them what I am like, you will assuredly do so.

Because self will disappear, be cast out.

When self has gone then those who see you will not see the self in you; only the ambassador of your King.

You have here in this seemingly narrow life of yours countless opportunities of overcoming self. Let this be your great task.

Wise Rest   February 4

REST should play a large part in the lives of My followers, for tiredness and physical strain can cause man to lose his consciousness of My Presence.

Then the Light that banishes evil seems to be withdrawn—never by deliberate act of Mine, but as the result of man's attitude towards Me. Ponder on this.

The Aching Spirit   February 5

JUST as I said that those who hungered and thirsted after righteousness would be filled, so I say to you—none ever longed to know Me better and remained unsatisfied. Even with your imperfect knowledge, you are daily realising how true this is.

Man dwells so much on material things that he fails to grasp the Spiritual laws that never fail.

For all spirit-longing there is fulfilment. I soothe the aching Spirit.

You think I answer your prayer. Yes, but the answer was *there*, awaiting the prayer.

You will see these simple Truths more and more as you live with Me; truths hidden from the wise but revealed to the little ones of the Kingdom.

True Humility   February 6

If I, your Lord and Master, have washed your feet, you ought also to wash one another's feet.

How My followers have misunderstood this. They interpret the required attitude to be one of service. In service there can be condescension, there can be a total lack of humility.

I sought to teach a lesson to those who would approach Me to partake of that wonderful Union with Me, vouchsafed to those who worthily eat of My Flesh and drink of My Blood.

I desired to teach them that they must come to Me *in the Spirit of humility towards others*. No sense of superiority, especially Spiritual superiority. True humility. Learn this lesson in daily Companionship with Me. "For I am meek and lowly of heart."

The Way of Progress   February 7

IMPRESS upon all that growth is one of the laws of My Kingdom.

However long your span of life on earth, it can never be too long for growth and progress.

Be ever seeking My Will for you. Not a new religion, nor the right religion, but—My Will. Then all will be well and growth will follow.

Future All Unknown February 9

PROBE not into the future. Prophecies are not for you. Be a humble follower in the crowd. Live with Me. Ponder My Words, My Teaching, My Actions.

Soon you will find that more and more opportunities of speaking of Me will present themselves. Do not make them. They will proceed from the pressure of inward growth, and not from outward stress.

All Will Be Well February 9

IN humble anticipation—wait.

Wait as a servant anticipating orders. Wait as a lover eager to note a need, and to supply it.

Wait for My Commands; wait for My Guidance; wait for My Supply. All will come.

In such a life you may well be of good cheer. Can a life be dull when always there is that watchful expectancy, anticipation of glad surprise, that wonder of fulfilment, that Joy of full supply?

Your Power February 10

IN your hands I have placed a wonderful force against evil. You cannot realise as yet the mighty weapon you wield.

Make known the Power of Prayer. A force so wonderful, so miracle-working, that when it is united with a will that seeks only My Will and with a Friendship with Me that calms, ennobles and enriches, then nothing can withstand its Power.

No Remorse   February 11

I SEEK to save you not only from falling into sin, but from the overwhelming remorse that follows the realization of sin.

I know that for frail man this is too great a burden. So when you let it overwhelm you, you nullify My saving Power.

I seek to save you from oppression and depression too. I bid you leave all to follow Me. That is, leave the sins and the failures of the past.

Out of the shadow into the sunlight of My Love and Salvation you must go.

See Me Everywhere Still   February 12

SEE Me in all your daily life.

See Me in the little happenings. Recognize me as the source of every act of kindness and Love.

Feel My Power with you when you face any task or danger. Know My consoling tenderness in every sorrow and disappointment.

I, the Master-Painter, can work into the ordinary colours of beauty until you see the befitting background for the joy and ecstasy of the radiance I give.

ABIDE secure in My friendship.

A friend who knows you through and through; knows all your pitiful attempts at living for Me, your many and tragic failures, your childish misunderstanding of Me and what I would do for you.

Your desire to serve Me, your clinging to Me in the dark hours of helplessness; your stumbling confidence in your efforts to walk alone—I know all.

I have seen your persistent blindness to My guidance; I have seen how you obstruct the answers to your own prayers; I have noted your easy acquiescence to those forces that oppose My loving purposes.

I know all this, and yet I say again: Abide with Me secure in My friendship.

Thanks for All February 14

THANK Me for all the withholding as well as for the giving. Thank Me for sunshine and rain, for drought and springs of water, for sleep and wakefulness, for gain and loss. Thank Me for all.

Know beyond all doubt, all fear, that all is well. Cling to Me in moments of weakness. Cling still in moments of strength, imploring that you may never feel self-sufficient.

No evil shall befall you, rest in this knowledge.

Green Pastures February 15

AFTER each salutary experience of life, each blow

it may deal you, separate yourself from the world for a time. Walk in My Green Pastures, and wander with Me beside the Waters of Comfort, until your soul is restored.

This is necessary so that you may readjust yourself to life. For you are a new being; you have had a new experience. Learn a new lesson. Your Union with Me will be the closer for your experience.

This is the time when My Love can whisper new meanings to you, can make the Friendship between us a closer, more holy Union.

Come with your Lover into the stillness of My Green Pastures, and walk with Me beside hushed waters.

He Changeth Not   February 16

MARK My Changelessness.

If I am truly the same, yesterday, to-day, and for ever, then I am no God of moods as so often man portrays Me. Can you worship a God swayed this way and that at man's demand?

Dwell upon the thought of My Changlessness until you grasp the Truth that only as *man* changes and comes within the influence of My unchanging Law of Love can he realize and experience the Power and Love I have unchangingly for all mankind.

Practise Peace   February 17

PEACE must fill your hearts and lives, and then you will find that ills and difficulties and sorrows and changes leave you unmoved. Practise that steadfast immobility, no matter what may threaten.

This spirit of calm trust is the shield that turns aside the darts and stings of adversity. Practise it.

Then you must seek to abide at the heart of the Universe with Me, at the centre with Me. There alone is changelessness and calm WITH ME.

The Perfect Pattern   February 18

See that thou make all things according to the pattern that was shown thee on the Mount.

OTHERWISE it would have been better not to have gone up the Mount at all? Take this lesson to heart. In your daily valley-life you must live out what you learn in the alone-time on heights with Me.

The Spirit-pattern is so glorious because it is made to fit your life, specially planned for you.

Obeying the command made Moses the good leader he became. This is the time, then, humbly to see your weakness, to adjust your life to the work of My Kingdom, to prepare to live in all things according to the pattern that was shown you on the Mount.

Youth Renewed   February 19

THEY that wait upon the Lord shall renew their strength.

To discover the Pearl of Great Price is to renew your youth.

The Kingdom of Heaven is a kingdom of perennial youth.

The Secret of Joy   February 20

SUCH rapture is yours. Count it all Joy to know Me, and to delight in Me. The secret of Joy is the longing to have My Will, and the gratification of that longing.

There is nothing in Heaven that transcends the Joy, the ecstasy, of loving and doing My Will. To a soul who realizes this wonder, Heaven is already attained as far as mortal here can attain it. My Will for you is My joyous arranging for you.

The frustration of the Divine Plan is man's tragedy.

Wise as Serpents   February 21

EACH servant of Mine should regard himself as an outpost for My Truths, where he must be prepared to receive My Messages, and to signal them on. This is work of great importance in My Kingdom.

Wherever you go make Me known. That was My Risen injunction, My Commission. Wherever you go establish outposts of My Empire, make contacts for Me. Make Me known to men—sometimes by speech, sometimes in silence.

Wonder-Work   February 22

ALL work with Me is wonder-work. God working in and through man. This should be the normal work of every Christian's day. For this I came to earth, to show man this could be.

For this I left the earth, so that this should be. Can life offer anything more for you than that you fulfil in yourselves My expectations for My disciples?

Satan frustrates My plan by whispering to My followers a mock humility in which they trace not his evil hand—"They are too weak, too small, too unimportant to do much . . ."

Away with false humility, which limits not you but Me. Mine is the Power.

Conquering and to Conquer   February 23

ALWAYS seek some conquest, for spiritual growth requires it. In the natural world you see how necessary this striving is, and in the mental and spiritual worlds there must be struggle too.

So, as you go forward in your spiritual life, you will see always a fresh conquest demanding your effort.

Shun stagnation. Never be discouraged if always you see some fault requiring to be overcome, some obstacle to be surmounted.

Thus you go forth with Me conquering and to conquer.

Always Antagonism   February 24

And He passing through the midst of them.

FACE evil undaunted, and it will fall back, and let you pass on and do your work for Me.

The maddened crowd had sought to cast Me

headlong, but they made way for Me, and through their midst I passed unhindered.

Do not be surprised to find antagonism where you meet evil, because you are a home of My Spirit, and it is My Spirit that arouses the antagonism. Go on your way so quietly, and trust in Me.

In My Strength My follower need not flinch, but, boldly facing evil, will overcome evil with good.

You follow the dauntless Christ.

The War Within   February 25

And he was dumb, because he believed not.

THERE is physical correspondence to faith and to doubt.

Especially is this so among those who would serve Me. For unlike others, they are not so controlled by the law of physical success or failure, but are under the direct control of the Laws of My Kingdom.

So, in many cases, you may note good health in one ignorant of Me, and ill-health in one of My followers, until he has learned the full control of the physical by the Spiritual. In his case the warring of physical and Spiritual may *cause* physical ill-health, or unrest.

So do not fret about the physical side, aim increasingly at control by My Spirit.

As from Me February 26

TAKE every little kindness, every faithful service, every evidence of thought and of Love—as from Me.

As you, and those who live with and for Me, show loving-kindness to others, because you are actuated by My Spirit, so you draw contacts into the circle of My ever-widening Spirit influence.

This is unfailingly so. It is a spiritual law. Though no word of Me may be spoken, yet in this way souls *are* attracted until at length they find Me, the centre and inspiration of all.

Well did I urge My Followers to become fishers of men. No great oratory or personality is needed for this soul-rescue work. Just follow Me as little children.

My Tireless Search February 27

SHARE with Me the tireless search for the lost, the ache of disappointment, the sublime courage, the tenderness of complete forgiveness. Share the Joys, the sorrows, the Love, the scorn.

I walk the lakeside still, and pause, as, to one and another, I utter the same call I uttered in Galilee, "Come and I will make you fishers of men."

The Simple Life February 28

THE Gift of Eternal Life is a most precious one. Each one who receives it must demonstrate by Joy and Trust and radiancy of Spirit, expressed in being and in bearing, the quality of the Life he possesses.

The other life is existence—just not death.

Power and Joy must radiate from you. These are the expressions of Eternal Life. Life Eternal is to know the Father and Me, His Son, Whom He sent.

"God so Loved the world that He gave His only Begotten Son that whosoever believeth on Him should not perish but have everlasting (*i.e.*, Eternal) Life."

Directly that Life is possessed by a man, all that is not simple, child-like has to go.

Not by complicated devices is My work accomplished.

My followers must be simple and direct. "Let your yea be yea and your nay be nay," I said.

Simplicity is forceful. Simplicity is great. It is a conquering Power.

UP-HILL

Does the road wind up-hill all the way?
Yes, to the very end.
Will the journey take the whole long day?
From morn to night, my friend.

C. G. Rossetti.

MARCH

Arise from Defeat March 1

IT is not upon one battle alone that all depends, or there would be no hope for My failures.

You enter upon a long campaign when you enter My army. Is the battle lost? Acquaint yourself with the cause, discover your weakness, and with dauntless faith, go forth resolved this time to conquer.

No man can conquer who has not learned his weakness, not made ready for the next conflict, and who does not know and claim and trust My strength, always available when summoned, as you have already proved.

Complete in Me March 2

A ROCK of Defence. A Joy to the saddened. A Rest to the weary. Calm to the ruffled.

A Companion of the sunlit glades. A Guide through the deserts of life. An Interpreter of experience. A Friend. A Saviour.

All these and many more would I be to you. Never a heart's need that I could not soothe and satisfy.

Search the ages. Many men have been many things to other hearts, but never one man to all men, never one man all to one man. This only the Maker of hearts could be.

Not only so, but in Me the soul finds its completion.

Shining Through   March 3

As you grow like Me so My Love must reflect more and more through you, Divinity and Majesty.

Sublime thought, yes, but you doubt if this can be. But God is Love, so God is Majesty. Thus gradually into the lives of those who follow Me there comes My Dignity and Majesty.

Have you not traced it in My closest friends?

To the Water's Edge   March 4

As God was in the days of Moses, so is He to-day. Responsive to the prayer of faith. Still ready and willing to make a path through the Red Sea.

Have the faith of Moses, who never faltered in his trust, even with the sea before, the advancing host behind, and no visible way of escape. *To the very edge of the waters he led his people.*

His task was done. It was for God, his God, in whom he trusted, to act now. Moses waited for, and expected, that act. But to the edge he had to go.

How often man draws back, halts at the thought of the troubled sea ahead. To go further is useless, he says, and gives up.

Or he goes within sight of the sea, and pauses. He must go on, always as far as he can; he must do all his share. God will not. On—*to the Edge of the Sea.*

Learn from this a mighty lesson. Do all your work, and leave your salvation to God. To say it will be no good is not to go to the edge, and that is to miss the saving Power of God.

The waters shall be divided, and you shall walk through the midst of the sea on dry land. I have said it. I, the Lord. Have I not done this for so many in your own day? For you? Think on these things.

"Share, Share" — March 5

I AM your Lord. Obey Me in all. You are being surely led into prosperity and true peace.

Let many share in your every gain. There must be no hoarding in the Christ-life. Not what you can gain, but what you can give. Keep your eyes fixed on Me. Seek to know My Will. Share. Share.

I am a Risen Lord. You cannot live with Me without partaking of My Risen Life. My Kingdom is sharing.

I must share all I have with My followers. So you, too, must share all that I give you—material and Spiritual Blessings—with others.

Your Circle Widens — March 6

As the circle of your life widens you will feel ever more and more the need of Me. The need indeed to draw from My unfailing resources to gain the help and wisdom required to deal with these new contacts.

Do not refuse them, only let nothing idle or of little worth engross your attention.

As your circle is enlarged, your means to deal with it adequately must grow too.

This is My desire. Ever walk with Me. Learn of Me. Witness for Me, Glorify Me.

How Firm Your Foundation   March 7

As one in a storm needs to dwell in quiet thought upon the firmness of the foundation of his home, so you need in dangers and difficulties of whatever kind to withdraw, and in quiet assurance dwell upon that foundation upon which the house of your life and character is built.

Rest your thoughts on this, on Me. Do not dwell on the channels through which My Help may be directed to you. To do so is indeed to feel at the mercy of wind and weather. You can draw no strength from such.

No, a sense of security can only come from relying on Me, the All-powerful, the Unchanging.

Security engenders Strength, then Peace, then Joy.

"Other foundations can no man lay."

New Life   March 8

ETERNAL Life gives a youthful resiliency.

Think of My parable of the wine-skins. Those who merely worship Me as a creed are like unto old wine-skins.

They cannot accept new truth, new life. It would destroy, not increase their faith.

Those who have My Gift of Eternal, youth-giving Life have the ever-expanding, revitalising, joy-quality of that Life.

The new wine poured so freely into new bottles. That bracing wine sustains the many who receive it.

Bear One Another's Burdens   March 9

Do not judge of another's capacity by your own.

If the burden another bears presses too heavily, what matter that you could bear that load lightly?

You must learn of Me to judge of the sorrow or strain of another, not with a feeling of superiority, but with one of humble thankfulness.

Would not *your* burdens have seemed light to Me? But insofar as they pressed heavily upon you so did I judge of them.

That which tore your heart may seem light to another.

Truly I said—Judge not. Only to God can the heart of man be made plain.

Seek My Presence, not only that you may understand Me, but that you may gain the insight to understand more clearly My other children.

Turn It to Good   March 10

NEVER flinch. My standard-bearers must you ever be. Bear your standard high.

Life has its dangers and difficulties, but real as these seem, the moment you see in them a power of evil that will in response to your faith be forced to work in some way for your good, in that moment of recognition evil and danger cease to have any power over you.

This is a wonderful truth. Believe it. Rejoice in it.

Accept Your Task   March 11

TAKE life as a task; each step of it to be practised until it can be done perfectly, that is, with patience, with soul harmony, and rest.

Remember the Christ of the humble ways is with you. His "Well done, good and faithful servant," is spoken, not to the great of earth but to the humble bearer of pain and annoyance, to the patient worker in life's ways of service.

So even on the quietest day, and in the lowliest way, mighty opportunities are given you of serving the King of Kings. See that you welcome and do not resent these opportunities.

The Springs of Love   March 12

BE gentle to all.

Drink of the Living water, deep draughts from the inexhaustible wells into which the very springs of Eternal Life flow from the Hills of God.

Think thoughts of Love and Beauty. Know no limit to all you can possess and be and do. Live in My Love; surrounded by It, blessed by It, shedding It bountifully on all about you, ever conscious of It being present with you.

You are here to reflect It.

Seek to see the good in all you meet—and in those of whom you hear.

You Are Complete   March 13

BE happy in Me. Feel that your life is complete in Me. Know the Joy of a friendship in which those who love Me share.

Know a glad contentment in the security of your protected and guided life. Value the Power that Union with Me gives you.

The greatest power that money, fame or position of the world can give, still leaves the possessor but as a child beating helpless hands against an impregnable fortress, as compared with the Power of My Spirit, which can render a follower of Mine himself an invincible, an all-conquering force.

Your Weak Point   March 14

"Be not overcome of evil, but overcome evil with good."

THE instruments in your hand for good are invincible against evil, did you but use them.

Every evil you face boldly, in My Spirit, flees at once, ashamed. No evil can look good in the face. Teach to all—that good is stronger than evil. You must answer the challenge of evil.

This spiritual warfare must be ceaselessly waged by My followers. Remember it is not where you are strongest that evil will attack you, but at your weak points. Hence the need to overcome. Be ready to see a weakness in yourself, and attack that until you are victor.

Guidance IS Guidance

BE still before Me. How often in a crisis man rushes hither and thither. Rush is a sign of weakness. Quiet abiding is a sign of strength.

A few quiet actions, as you are led to do them, and all is accomplished wisely and rightly, more quickly and more effectually than could be done by those who rush about and act feverishly.

Guidance IS Guidance, the being led, the being shown the way. Believe this.

Softly, across life's tumult, comes the gentle Voice, "Peace, be still." The waves of difficulty will hear. They will fall back. There will be a great calm.

And then the Still Small Voice of Guidance.

Perfect Everything

Be ye therefore perfect, even as your Father in Heaven.

THAT was the aim I set before My disciples when I spoke to them on the Mount.

That is the aim I set before you and every follower of Mine to-day.

To *achieve* this you would be as God.

To *aim at less* would mean an unworthy standard.

To keep your gaze on this as your standard means that your eyes are fixed on the Heights of God, always directed above the difficulties and the lower aims and desires and standards of others round you.

47

Blessed are they that hear My Voice.

DEAF to My Voice man can so often be. Live, My children, more in the Unseen World. There, in the contemplation of Me, your whole nature becomes sensitive to My faintest whisper.

I have told you, I tell you again, the Unseen World is the real world. Realise more and more as you go through this earth-life that this is only a material-plane parenthesis. The real paragraph, chapter, book of Life is the Spirit-Life.

This point of view will alter your idea of suffering, failure, and the work of life here. It will give you a new view of death. Birth begins the parenthesis, death closes it. Then back to real Life-History. Absorb this.

When you have done so, you will get that same idea about the various periods of your earth-life. Times of struggle, defeat, joy, failure, work, rest, success—Treat them all as parts of a parenthesis in the one Eternal Life of *spiritual progress.*

Joy from Sorrow   March 18

I BIND up the broken hearts with the cords wherewith men scourged Me in the Judgment Hall, with the whips of scorn wherewith men have mocked My Love and Divinity down the ages.

Symbol, this, of the way in which, out of seeming obstacles stepping-stones can be fashioned, and, out of trials undreamt-of, blessings can be wrought.

Share My Life with its longings and tears, with its Joys unspeakable and its heartaches beyond human description.

Share My Joy

Through the Archway   March 19

By the obedience of one shall many be made righteous.

OBEDIENCE is the keystone of your arch of worship. On it depends your Love and Power.

Through that archway shall many pass into My Holy Place. Once therein their questing souls will pass into My Holy of Holies. Is it too much to ask of you obedience that this may be accomplished?

Do not fret that your life is lived in lowly places. It is not to be lived to impress this earth-plane, but to be so faithful and obedient that those for whom you desire much, shall have THAT much impressed upon them on the spirit-plane.

That much, and more, than you can desire for them.

First Place   March 20

I DO not promise My followers the world's ease and pleasures. I promise those Joys that the world can neither give nor take away.

I promise the heart-rest found with Me alone.

It does not mean that all the beauties and pleasures of the world must be renounced, but that they must be enjoyed only after the treasures and

Joys of My Kingdom have been learned, appreciated and given first place.

Simplicity   March 21

BE content to do the simple things.

Never think that if you have not the cleverness of the world I cannot use your services.

Pure sparkling wine may be in a silver goblet or in a simple glass, but, to the one who receives, it is the wine that matters, not the vessel, provided that be pure and clean.

It is My truth that matters, not the person that utters it, provided the desire is there to deliver My Message for ME.

True simplicity is found only as you live in Me and act in My Strength; for only in our close companionship can real value be achieved.

Never accept the values of earth. Be content with simplicity.

Love's Overflow   March 22

I DESIRE the love of man's heart in abundant measure.

Not because God would be adored for Himself and for His own gratification, but because I know that only as the love of man flows out to Me does man attain to his purest and best.

That rush of love, which follows the understanding and realization of My Love for man, sweetens and purifies his whole being.

"Thou shalt love thy neighbour as thyself."

The love you give to your neighbour is the *over-flow* of your love to Me

No Personalities   March 23

DEAL with each difficulty as you must.

Then live above it. Say "In Him I conquered." The fight is ever between you and evil, never between you and another. *Never make it a personal matter.*

If you are fighting with the weapons of the world—envy, resentment, anger—you cannot use those of My Kingdom—Prayer, Love, Peace—which would give you a God-given conquering strength.

It is the endeavour to call both God and mammon to your aid that makes for lack of success. The world looks on in scornful pity, and My followers themselves doubt and wonder.

So often they do not see their own error, but attribute to suffering for My Sake that which may not be according to My Will.

If It Offends—   March 24

QUESTION yourself as to your weakness. What caused your failure? To continue to bemoan your folly is in itself a weakness. My followers must be strong, not in themselves, but in Me.

The look at Self, however penitent, cannot give strength.

Look unto Me, and, whatever the seeming sacrifice, be ruthless with what hindered or caused you to fall.

Sift Your Motives March 25

WALK in My Ways. Follow the path I have bidden you tread.

Humble yourselves before Me, and keep My laws, so shall you have perfect peace.

I am with you to give you the needed strength. Go forward unafraid. Grow in Grace, and in the knowledge of Me, your Master and your Friend. Count all the learning of earth's wisest as nothing compared with the wisdom that I, your Lord, would show you.

Love and learn. You have much, very much to do for My Kingdom. So seek to become perfect. Sift your motives. All that is unworthy cast aside, uproot its inner growth.

You are freely forgiven. Forgive freely, largely, wonderfully.

Keep Step March 26

Go forward, glad indeed.

Walk with Me until your faltering, flagging footsteps learn to keep in step with Me, and gain a firmness and a confidence unknown before.

Walk with Me until a gladsome rhythm reveals the conquest-spirit that you draw from Me, and your whole being thrills with the joy of being, doing and even suffering with Me.

Thus in loving Communion with Me you learn to know My needs and My wishes for others.

"Here am I, Lord, send me" shows very surely a child-like eagerness, the eagerness of love, even the eagerness for adventure for My cause.

For in My Secret Service there is surely the thrill of *adventure*.

Spirits in Training March 27

Go on along the highway of the Kingdom until all that comes, that touches your outward lives and circumstances, has no power to ruffle your spirit-calm. Make it a delight so to train yourselves.

Why does man rebel at aught that should teach him poise of spirit, whilst in the physical world he welcomes severe exercise that would increase his powers?

The children of this world are surely wiser in their generation than the children of light. If My Children of Light gave to their spirit and character-training all the care that the children of this world give to the body—its feeding, its clothing, its wellbeing—how rapid would their spiritual progress be!

Yet how little does the body matter compared with the growth of the Spirit. "Fear not them that kill the body, but are not able to kill the soul."

In Eternity Now March 28

HEIRS of God. Joint heirs with Me of Eternal Life, if so be that you suffer with Me, that we may also be glorified together.

Glory denotes perfection of character. This can only be learned as you allow discipline to play its part in your life, and also as you entrust your sinful past to Me.

Perfect through suffering. You cannot escape

discipline and be truly My disciple.

If you think that life is too short for all you have to do and to conquer, then remember that you have already entered upon ETERNITY.

The True Sign   March 29

How many believed on My Name after seeing the signs which I did?

Not for the signs, not for the water made wine, not for My miracles will My true follower believe in Me.

No, for something deeper, seen only with the eyes of faith, realized only by a heart of love responding to My Heart of Love. Not of these must it be said, "I do not trust Myself unto them" as I did of those who saw My signs.

I must trust Myself and My Cause to My followers who see me with the eyes of faith. How else can I be loved and known?

They will meet Me, the outcast Saviour, when I am performing no mighty deeds, wandering unheeded and unacclaimed through dark and lonely ways, and they will pause, all other pursuit forgotten, and will yet turn and follow Me.

Follow because of some chord in them responsive to the yearning of My Heart for Man, who has shut Me out. Follow, too, because of that in Me which is responsive to the cry of man's hungering soul.

The Love of Your Life   March 30

I AM beside you. I am with you in all that you do.

I control your thoughts, inspire your impulses, guide your footsteps.

> I strengthen you, body, mind and spirit.
> I am the link between you and those who are in the Unseen.
> I am the Love of your lives.
> Controller of your destinies.
> Guardian, advocate, provider, Friend.

Yes, love Me more and more. So will you not only enjoy to the full the treasures and pleasures of My Kingdom, but increasingly those of Nature, My gift to My world.

The Wrong Voice   March 31

I AM the Great Teacher, so ready to explain the simplest lesson to the most ignorant.

It is not for you to seek everywhere explanations of Me and My Kingdom, its laws and its purposes.

Learn of Me. How often would I have spoken to some heart, but the voice of one too eager with explanations about Me crowded Me out.

When Andrew brought Simon to Me *he* was silent to let his brother learn of *Me*.

The reason for this crowding out of My Voice by My disciples is their unwillingness to believe that I *do* speak to-day. So, thinking they worship a silent Christ, they seek to make amends by *their* much speaking.

> "*To Thee our morning song of praise,*
> *To Thee our evening prayer we raise.*"

The Time of Resurrection

SPRING brings its message of Hope.

Not only does it proclaim the Truth that Nature arises from her time of decay and darkness to a new life. But, My children, it surely speaks to the individual, to nations, to My world, that the time of decay and darkness for them too can pass, and that from conflict and storm, disaster and sin they can spring to a new and gladdening Resurrection-Life.

But Nature obeys My Laws. It is by her obedience that the quickening of new life is succeeded by the beauty of Risen Power.

So, only as man obeys My Will and works according to My Divine Plan for him can harmony follow chaos, peace follow war, and a reign of Love succeed one of conflict and carnage.

Resurrection Preparation

I AM the Master of the Universe. Accept My ordered Word. When you do this in joyful sincerity, you link yourself with all creative force of the Universe.

My Spirit can then be operative, first *in* you and then *through* you.

My followers forget that the scourging at the pillar, the Divine control ("He answered never a word") and the Cross, man-rejected, man-forsaken, all these preceded the Resurrection.

Without these there could have been no Resurrection. These steps in Spirit-conquest had to be, before My all-powerful, Divine Spirit could be released to be for ever available for those who would hear My Call, and would will to walk in My Way.

See Them Free   April 3

IF I bore the sins of all in My agonised Heart in the Garden of Gethsemane and on Calvary, then when you seek to punish others whom you despise, you punish and despise Me.

My throwing aside the grave-clothes, and My stepping out into that sunlit Garden on Easter Morn were symbolic of the freedom I had bought for My children, and which they would know in Me.

Are you seeking to bind the grave-clothes round Me? When you recognize a man's sins you must go further always and see him as free, the grave-clothes of sin and limitation cast aside; the stone, that shut out his Vision of Love and God, rolled away; he, a risen man, walking in My Strength, and conquering in My Power.

Sharing My Burden   April 4

REMEMBER the Truth that you are learning, even now, though dimly.

In Eternal Life there are no time-limits. So My sacrifice was for you to-day, this hour, as truly as

57

ever it was for those who watched Me on Calvary.

I am the changeless One. The same yesterday and for ever. Sacrificing Myself to-day, rising to-day. You then, once you embrace Eternal Life, enter into My Suffering, and help to carry My Cross, as truly to-day as if you had walked beside Me to Calvary.

Redeemed   April 5

AGONY and heartache, pain and loneliness, such as no human being has ever known, were the price of your redemption.

Truly you are not your own.

You are bought with a price. You belong to Me.

You are Mine to use, Mine to love, Mine to provide for.

Man does not understand the infinite Love of the Divine. Man teaches that as I bought him, so he has to serve, obey and live for Me.

He fails to understand that because he is Mine, bought by Me, it is My responsibility to supply his every need. His part is to realize My ownership and to claim my Love and Power.

The Veil Has Gone   April 6

And the veil of the Temple was rent in twain, from the top to the bottom.

THE veil that had hidden God from the knowledge and sight of man was at last removed.

I, God and man, had torn away the veil separating God the Father, and man, My brother. I came to reveal the Father to man, and I live, ever live, to make intercession to the Father for man. I am the Great Mediator between God and man, the Man, Christ JESUS.

Bear Reproach Gladly April 7

REST unto your souls is found at My Feet. The place of rest is the place of humility.

When you rejoice to serve humbly, when you are content for men to think ill of you, when you can bear reproach and scorn gladly, then what can disturb the gladness of your soul, its rest?

No unrest can assail and hurt the soul that has not its spring in self. That self must be nailed to My Cross, that self must die before you can truly say—"I live, yet not I, but Christ liveth in me."

Stones Rolled Away April 8

And they saw that the stone was rolled away.

How needless their questioning among themselves had been:—

"Who shall roll away the stone?"

Wherever My followers go full of desire to do Me loving service, they shall find the stones of difficulty, of obstruction, rolled away.

They came, these faithful women, to the sepulchre with the spices and ointments they had prepared.

Come, too, with your spices of Love to do Me

service, and you shall find you have been anticipated. I am ever eager in Love to do you service.

The Life Glorious April 9

*If by the Spirit you mortify the flesh,
you shall live.*

THIS is a further progress-step in My Kingdom.
The flesh must hold no pleasure for you that is not
held in leash, always under subjection to the Spirit.

It was the utter subjection of the flesh that was
manifested in My Silence at the pillar, and in the
face of the jibes and insults and blows. It was this
complete subjection which meant a Risen Body.

Resurrection-faith is not a matter of belief in
Me, and in My Power working a miracle, it is a
faith in Me and My Power leading to entire subjection of the body.

The body completely under control of the
Spirit *is* a Risen Body. See now the importance of
self-discipline.

Break Free April 10

I SENT no disciple to carry My Healing Power to
the Syrophœnician woman's sick daughter, the
centurion's servant, or to the ruler's son. My Word
was all-sufficient.

All that I needed was the faith of the petitioner.
Can you not realize that?

Learn to understand and to ask more of Me. If
you do not, then others' bonds are your responsibility.

Loose your own body from all bonds. Remember "the beam and the mote."

As the fault (the beam) is removed from your own eye, giving you the power to remove the mote from your brother's eye, so if you bring your body into subjection, discipline it wholly, you will be enabled to free your brother from bonds that bind him to ill-health.

Easter Gladness   April 11

LOVE and Laugh. To the world, sad faces and depressed spirits speak of a buried Christ. If you want to convince men that I am Risen, you must go through life with Easter gladness. You must prove by your lives that you are Risen with Me.

Men will not learn of My conquest over death by the arguments of theologians, but by the lives of My followers, My Risen followers. If you are still wearing the grave-clothes of gloom and depression, of fear and poverty, men will think of us as tomb-bound still.

No, live in the Spirit of the Garden on that Easter morning. For you, too, I will roll away the stone from the door of the sepulchre. Walk unbound in the Garden with Me, in the Garden of Love, Joy, child-like, boundless Faith—the Garden of Delights.

Fair Delights   April 12

IT is My Pleasure that you wait before Me.

Companionship with Me, with its soul-rest, is all too often sacrificed for petition.

Be content awhile to be silent in My Presence. Draw in that Spiritual Power which will strengthen you to conquer the weaknesses you so deplore.

Life in Me is one of radiance.

Eternal Life is Life refreshed by Living Waters.

There is no stagnation in My Kingdom, in that place prepared for hearts that love Me.

It is a place of Fair Delights.

Claim what you will. It is yours.

Heaven's Almoner   April 13

IT may not be *your* need I am seeking to supply at a particular moment, but of another through you.

Remember what I have told you before: it is empty vessels I fill, into open hands that I place My supply.

Too often My followers are so busy clutching their foolish possessions that they have no hands to receive the larger blessings, the needed gifts, I am waiting to pass to them, and, through them, to others.

Help all to see the wonderful life that could open out before them. To be Heaven's almoner is the work to which I call each follower Mine.

You Can Do This   April 14

I WILL give you rest.

My Gift truly, but the result of your trust.

Train yourself to trust so completely that no tremor even of doubt or fear can enter in.

No fear of the future, no cloud over the present, no shadow of the past.

When the absence of fear is the result of strength for the way gained by contact with Me, and of complete reliance upon My Tenderness and My Power, then you have *My Gift of Rest*.

The Sunlit Way

KNOW that your Source of joy is something changeless. The hopes of the world are but in material things and when these pass or change their joy fades, hope dies, only dark night remains.

Speak comfort to such. Tell of My Love surrounding you, that My protecting Power is yours. That I can never fail one who trusts in Me. That you can breathe in courage from My Presence as you breathe in air.

Tell the world—that for one who walks a cheerless road with Me, the bare hedge doth blossom as the rose, and life is bathed in sunlit joy.

Regain Dominion

Let them have dominion.

MAN has lost this dominion because he failed to be guided by My Spirit. He was never meant to function alone. Body, mind and spirit, he was created by My Father.

The senses were given him to link him to earth, and to create and maintain contact with the world around; but the spirit was definitely his link for guidance and instruction from the world of My Kingdom.

He is a lost soul until he links up in this way, just as a man blind, deaf and dumb would be in a world of sense. This was man's fall. He had this power and lost it.

New Beauties   April 17

LIFE has so many lessons to teach you. You may not be able to travel through your material world. But for your spirit there are vast and beautiful realms in which you can be ever travelling and exploring; and, with ever-increasing capacity for enjoyment, discovering new beauties of Spiritual Truth.

God's Mosaic   April 18

LIFE is a journey. The choice as to who shall be your conductor is your own. Once that choice is made and you feel you have placed yourself in wise Hands, do not spoil your journey by frustrating the plans made for your comfort and happiness.

Rest content with the plans I have made for you. No detail has been too small for My loving consideration. Know that your lives are being truly God-conducted, and so will bring you the greatest happiness and success.

The greater the trust you repose in Me the wider will be My scope for the plans I have made for you.

Life is a mosaic planned by God. Each God-directed thought, impulse, and action of yours is necessary to the carrying out of the perfect design.

That design is of exquisite workmanship.

Love-Controlled   April 19

LIVE in My Love.

Return to Me ever for refilling, that your soul may breathe in and breathe out Love as your lungs breathe in and breathe out air.

There is nothing in you that creates Love, so how can you give it out unless you are receiving it?

All service, to be truly effective and of permanent value, must be wrought in Love. Where Love is, self cannot hold sway, and self nullifies the good in service.

See Me and My thought for you in all your daily life; so, conscious of My Love, you will absorb that Love until it permeates your whole being, and inspires and illumines all you do and say.

The Joyous War   April 20

LIVE much a life apart with Me. In the world but not of it. You can do this even in a crowd, provided self does not intrude.

It is a sign of progress that you cannot be indulging thoughts of self and then turn to Me in complete self-forgetfulness.

Your life must be one of intense service and consecration. Your fight is not so much an active one in the world, as one of active warfare on the un-

seen plane. A war truly against principalities and
and powers. Nevertheless a joyous war.

"How Oft in the Conflict"   April 21

> Lord, bid me come to Thee upon the
> waters.

"COME."

All that I did when on earth I do to-day in the
Spirit-realm.

My servant Paul realized this Truth when he
spoke of Me as the same yesterday, to-day, and
for ever.

When the faintest fear of all that lies before
you disturbs you, when you are conscious of the
loss of Spirit-buoyancy, then you are looking at
the waves and feeling the wind is contrary.

Then you cry, "Lord, save me, I perish."

And My Hand will be outstretched to save you
as it saved My fearful, doubting Peter.

Light Comes   April 22

"LORD, show me Thyself" is a cry that never goes
unanswered.

Not to physical vision comes the awareness, but
to spiritual insight, as more and more you realize
My Love, My Power and the manifold wonders
of My character.

Its Humility, its Majesty, its Tenderness, its
Sternness, its Justice, its Mercy, its Healing of
sore wounds, and its consuming Fire.

Man turns to books, he studies theology, he

seeks from other men the answer to life's riddles, but he does not come to Me.

Is there a problem?

Do not worry over its solution.

Seek Me. Live with Me. Talk to Me. Company with Me, daily, hourly. *Lo, suddenly you see.*

Words of Life   April 23

Lord, Thy Word abideth and our foot-steps guideth.

TREASURE My Words in your heart. They will meet your need *to-day* as surely as they met the needs of those to whom I spoke them when I was on earth for they were not spoken in time but in Eternity.

If My gift to man is Eternal Life, then the words inspired by that Life are eternal, appropriate to your needs to-day as they were then.

But the words and the guidance are not for all. They are for those who ACCEPT MY great gift of Eternal Life.

"And this is Life Eternal, that they might know Thee the only true God, and Jesus Christ, Whom Thou hast sent."

"Lord, Use Me, I Beseech Thee"   April 24

I WILL use you as you eliminate self and offer Me a consecrated personality, made in My Image.

There can be no limit to My power to use one such. Nothing is impossible to Me. My Love is limitless, My Tenderness is limitless, My Understanding is limitless.

Every attribute of the Godhead is complete, inexhaustible in a way you can only dimly see.

Your Limitations   April 25

THE words I give you mark steps in Spiritual Progress.

There can be no limit to the Spirit Power you may possess as self is turned out and My Will welcomed.

But to those who yield themselves wholly to Me there *are* limitations as far as the material is concerned, as only what will assist Spiritual growth or manifestation is for these. Yet all your needs will be supplied.

Vain Toil   April 26

Master, we have toiled all night and have taken nothing.

THERE will be nights of wearied anguish, when you toil and catch nothing.

There will be mornings of rapture when the result of your prayers and longings will be so great as to bring you to your knees with a humility born of a wonder of fulfilment—"the nets brake."

Share the loneliness with Me—the weariness, the dreariness, all with Me, as I share all with you.

Welcome Them   April 27

MORE and more I shall send into your life those whom you shall help. Have no fear. Do not doubt your wisdom to deal with them. It is My Wisdom that will help them, not any wisdom of yours.

Shower Love on all. Nothing will be too much that you can do for others. Delight in My Word, in My Love.

As you grow more conscious of that Love you will feel more and more the responsibility laid upon you to make that Great Love of My aching Heart known to those for whom I died, and for whom I ever live to make intercession.

Overshadowing Wings   April 28

My child, you are tired with the burden and heat of the day.

Stay awhile and know that I abide with you, and know that I speak Peace unto your soul.

Dread nothing, fear nothing. Know that all is well. The day is far spent. The toil has been long, but evening rest with Me is sweet.

The gathering gloom of night will be to your heart but the *overshadowing wings* of the Eternal God.

Deep in your heart you feel the striving of wonderful Truths. Faint sense of the Glory to be revealed.

No Message, But—   April 29

My child, wait before Me.

You may receive no message, but in this waiting time, even if you are not conscious of being taught, you are being changed.

The eye of your soul will be focussed upon Me

and the insight gained will be calming, remedial, strengthening.

My First Missionary   April 30

My denunciations were for the self-satisfied.

For the sinner, who felt his failure and weakness, I had the tenderest pity. "Go, and sin no more," was My Word to the woman taken in adultery.

But what a Word of hope that was, revealing as it did the assurance that I trusted her not to fall into sin again. That I deemed her capable of a new life.

The Samaritan woman at Sychar's well I trusted with a secret that even My disciples had not shared fully with Me. She was one of My first missionaries.

I recognized the wealth of love in the offering of the woman who was a sinner. There was no public denunciation of her sin, no repulse of her love.

> *"Holy Father, cheer our way*
> *With Thy love's perpetual ray;*
> *Grant us every closing day,*
> *Light at evening time."*

Bounteous Giving   May 1

NOT what you can gain in any situation, but what you can give must be your question. You follow Me, of Whom it was said, "Even Christ pleased not Himself." So love, so help, so serve.

Seek the weak and wandering. Care for all.

Realize My overflowing and overwhelming Bounty. The stores of the Lord are inexhaustible. But to test and prove My generosity fully you must be generous.

My lovers give with no niggard hands. A heart overflowing with gratitude for what it has received expends joyous gratitude in giving.

Peace Unto Your Souls   May 2

> *Peace I leave with you, My Peace give*
> *I unto you.*

I KNEW that only in Peace could My work be done. Only in Peace could My followers help souls to Me. At all costs keep that Peace. If your heart-peace is unruffled, then every thought is a mighty force for ME. Then every act is one of power.

Rely on My leading. Nothing is impossible to Me.

Unlimited expectancy yours. Unlimited power *Mine.*

Useless Activity   May 3

PREPARATION-time is so neglected by My followers. Consequently there is lack of power in work for Me.

To alter the laws of a country is no real remedy for ill. Men's hearts must be altered by contact with Me.

Remember the lessons I have taught you about useless activity. When most work cries out to be done, then it is truly the time—not to rush, but to Commune with Me and My Father.

Never feel strong in yourself. Know that only in My Strength can you accomplish all. No mountain of difficulty can then be insurmountable or immovable.

The Acceptable Gift   May 4

REST in My Love. Abide in Me.

Leave all to follow Me—your pride, your self-sufficiency, your fears of what others may think —All.

Have no fear. Go forth into the unknown with Me, fearful of nothing with so sure a convoy.

Just as a flower, given as an offering to a loved one, so is your tribute of love to Me.

As Mary gave her Love-offering, spikenard very precious, so give to Me your love and understanding.

Dangerous Channels   May 5

"SAVIOUR, let me be a channel for Thy Mighty Power."

First you must be kept by that Mighty Power.

For it must be a consecrated life to be so used.

My Power passing through wrong channels would work harm. It could not be.

The alloy of the channel would poison the Spirit-flood.

The Fertile Glade   May 6

Seek and you shall find.

As a mother hiding from her child puts herself in the way of being found, so with Me. So the finding of Me and of the treasures of My Kingdom may not always depend upon ardent intent securing attainment, but upon the mere setting out on the quest.

Is this a comfort to you?

When you set out upon a time of seeking I place Myself in your way, and the sometime arid path of prayer becomes a fertile glade in which you are surprised to find your search so soon over. Thus mutual Joy.

Clouds and Rain   May 7

SEE My goodness in the clouds and rain, as well as in the sunshine of life. Both express so wonderfully the goodness and love of your Lord.

Just as the shady glade, the cool riverside, the mountain-top, the blazing highway, all meet the varying needs of man.

The Dross and the Gold

SHARE your Joy with Me.

Tell Me of all that gladdens you throughout your day. I am near to hear. Feel that I alone share to the full your heart-thrills, because with Me no success of yours engenders regret nor is tinged with envy.

Is it not My Joy, My success, accomplished only in and through Me?

Share all with Me. The disappointment, not only in others but all too poignantly in yourself. Share your backward step as well as one of progress.

Bring all to Me, and together, in tender Love, we can sift the dross from the gold.

Come back to Me, ever sure of a welcome, ever glad to feel My Presence in and round you.

Call Me Often

SPEAK My Name often during the day. It has the power to banish evil, and to summon Good.

JESUS.

In Me dwelleth all the fulness of the Godhead, so that when you call Me you call to your aid all there is of Good to need.

Talk to Me

TALK to Me about the world's misunderstanding of Me. Tell Me that your Love will seek to comfort Me for that. Tell Me your life shall be devoted to bringing about an understanding between Me and those you meet who love Me not.

As one who knows a prisoner has been wrongly convicted devotes a life-time to the vindication of that loved one's name, and counts all the trials and troubles, misunderstandings and hardships encountered in so doing as nothing, so that his object is accomplished—let it be thus with you, longing to make Me known.

Bigger Demands   May 11

As your faith in Me grows and your sphere of influence extends, your claims will be the greater. Yet no real need of yours shall go unsatisfied.

You will make bigger demands, and ever more and more you will be trusting Me to supply the little wants. This trust will come as you realize My power more and more, and feel My Love and know its tender watchfulness in every detail of your daily life.

"Rejoice, again I say, Rejoice."

With a loved human friend a big gift may be prized as proof of a big love, but great devotion is displayed even more in the anticipation of the little wants, in the solicitude shown in little ways.

Delight in My Love, so shown.

Lord of Joy   May 12

THE UNSPEAKABLE JOY offered Himself for joyful recognition.

This is a further stage of development.

You enter upon it when you realize that I was the expression in time of the Joy of all Eternity. That joy I offered to all who would see in My way the path of Joy, and who would hail Me not only as the Man of Sorrows but as the Lord of Joy.

This truth becomes known to those only who give joyful recognition to this all-amazing, all-sustaining, all-revealing JOY.

Highways and Byways   May 13

THE way of Holiness differs for each of My followers as the character of each differs. My command for you is not necessarily My command for another.

My followers often forget this. Because I may have told them to take a certain road they are sure that you should be walking in the same way.

Heed them not. Remember, too, that a way of discipline for you may not be My will for another.

You Have Been Warned   May 14

FASTING is the starving out of self. It may not always be by food-abstinence. But it is an absolute essential of progress in the life with Me.

There is no standing still in the Christian life. If there is not progress there is retrogression.

I redeemed you. Bought you back from slavery to sin, of whatever kind.

So, when weakness overcomes you, and you yield to temptation, you make of My Redemption a mockery.

Grasp This Truth   May 15

Too many hinder their work for Me by seeking to

justify themselves. You are fighting for Christ the King, not for yourself. The explaining or justifying must be for Me.

In any difficulty with another put yourself in his place and pray that his difficulty may be solved for him.

This will bring about a solution of yours, and help you to see better that for which you should pray.

The power to realize the needs of those you contact can only be acquired by absorbing sympathy and understanding from My Life. So, time for knowing Me must be increasingly dear and necessary to you.

Your task is to show the Power of My Spirit working through a life of yielded will, and the Joy that transforms the life when this is so.

Hungry Hearts   May 16

We would see Jesus.

THIS is still the cry of a hungry, dissatisfied, seeking world.

I look to My followers to satisfy that cry.

Reflect Me, that the seekers may see Me in you, and then go on to company with Me.

Rejoice at this as John rejoiced when he could point his disciples to Me with the brave and humble words, "He must increase, and I must decrease."

Go on in Faith and Joy and Love.

My Messenger Goes Before May 17

WHEN you think of Me as your Rescuer, remember it is not only from sin, depression or despair.

It is from the difficulties of life also and from perplexity as to your path. I solve your problems. I provide the channel through which help will come.

I send My messenger to prepare your way before you. I train you so that you may be fitted for your next task, so that you may be worthy of My promised blessing. That blessing which I long to shower on you.

The Healing Light May 18

WHEREVER My followers go, *there* should be My Light surrounding them. The Light of the Sun of Righteousness.

Evil cannot live in that Light.

Man is only just learning that light banishes disease.

Every follower of Mine who is in close personal touch with Me is surrounded by this Light. Light Eternal. Light reflected by a consciousness of My Presence.

So whether he speak or not he must be the means of diffusing My Light wherever he goes.

The Ordered Life May 19

You cannot be doing My work well and wielding a worthy influence unless all your life is ordered.

Let that be your aim and your achievement.

Secure this order and you will be able to do so much more in My service, and, without haste or unrest, reflect more the order and beauty of My Kingdom.

You need this discipline in your life.

Peace is the result of an ordered life lived with Me.

Prepare yourself for each task, for each occasion. Pray for those you will contact, your time with them.

This will save discord, and will enable the work and planning, in which you co-operate with them, to be fruitful for good.

Spirit Waves   May 20

You have been told to end all prayer upon a note of praise.

That note of praise is not only faith rising up through difficulties to greet Me. It is even more. It is the Soul's recognition that My Help is already on the way.

It is the echo in your heart of the sound borne on Spirit Waves.

It is given to those who love and trust Me to sense this approach.

So rejoice and be glad, for truly your redemption draweth nigh.

Soften the Soil   May 21

In My story of the Sower the hearts that lost the blessing, that held no good result, lost it because My servants had failed to prepare the ground.

They had failed to guard those they sought to influence, against the power of evil, and hardness of heart. They had failed to brace them to bear trouble and difficulty. They had failed to warn them against becoming too engrossed with having and getting.

The ground of the Sower had not been prepared. Much prayer must precede seed-sowing if the labour is not to be in vain.

So seek to prepare My way before Me. Then I, the Great Sower, will come. Harvest will indeed be great.

Christianity Has Not Failed   May 22

MEN are trying to live the Christian Life in the Light and Teaching of My three years' Mission alone. That was never My Purpose.

I came to reveal My Father, to show the God-Spirit working in man. I taught, not that man was only to attempt to copy the JESUS of Nazareth, but that man was also to be so possessed by My Spirit, the Spirit actuating all I did, that he would be inspired as I was.

Seek to follow Me by the Power of the In-dwelling Spirit which I bequeathed to you. This Spirit WILL guide you into all Truth.

I told My disciples that I could not tell them all but the Spirit would guide them. That is where My followers fail Me. Dwell more and more upon this Spirit-Guidance, promised to all, and so little claimed.

Getting and Giving

COME, My children, come and gladly claim. Come and take from Me. Come with outstretched hands to receive.

And keep nothing. Eagerly pass on My gifts so that I may again bless your emptiness and refill your vessels.

You begin to understand this Law of Supply.

Man does not realize that for the children of the Kingdom the law is not that which rules outside.

My followers must be channels through which My gifts can pass to others. You cannot obtain My supply and follow the way of the world.

No Separation

Come to Me.

AT first with reluctant footsteps, then, as our Friendship grows, ever more and more eagerly, until the magic of My Presence not only *calls* but *holds* you, and reluctantly you turn to earth's ways and duties again.

But, as time passes, even that reluctance passes too, as you know there is no separation, not even a temporary one, in such Companionship; because I go with you and My Words you carry ever in your heart.

New Temptations

YOU will find that as you grow in Grace evil forces are more ready to hinder your work and influence.

Walk warily, watchfully.

Always see that there is a new discipline to become a part of your armour, for as you progress new temptations will present themselves.

In rarefied air there are subtle dangers unknown in the valley or on the lower sides of the mountain. Many a disciple fails because he is not aware of the mountain dangers.

A Day at a Time   May 26

THE problems of to-morrow cannot be solved without the experience of to-day.

There is a plan for your lives dependent upon the faithful work of each day. You frustrate that plan if you leave to-day's task incomplete, while you bestir and fret yourself over to-morrow's happenings.

You will never learn the Law of Supply if you do this, and the learning of that Law is the lesson for now.

Home of Content   May 27

CAN you not trust My supply?

All is yours. Could I plan your journey, your way of life, your work and not count the cost?

Can you not trust Me even as you would trust an earthly friend? Live in My Kingdom and then the supply of the Kingdom is yours.

I wish you to learn the Glory of a God-protected life.

No idle, fruitless rushing hither and thither.

Storms may rage, difficulties press hard, but you

will know no harm . . . safe, protected and guided.

Love knows no fear.

Care for All   May 28

REALIZE My overflowing and overwhelming Bounty. The stores of the Lord are inexhaustible, but to test My generosity to the full you must be generous.

My lovers give with no niggard hands.

Cares Cared For   May 29

Casting all your care upon Him, for He hath care of you.

How precious these words. Care, attention, and the Love which prompts them, are all indicated here, as also the most tender provision.

You are not told to put your worries away merely so that you may forget about them, but to cast them upon God. That is different: they will be dealt with.

Difficulties will be cleared away, mistakes rectified, weaknesses remedied, disease healed, problems solved.

See Clear   May 30

YOUR power to help your brother does not depend upon him: it is in your own hands. It is conditional upon your casting out the beam out of your own eye.

Attack not your brother's faults but your own.

As you eradicate those you discover where your brother needs help, and you acquire the power to give him that help to conquer and to eradicate his faults.

Into My Likeness   May 31

"CHANGED . . . from Glory to Glory." Changed from one character to another. Each change marking as it were a milestone on the Spiritual Highway.

The Beauty of the view you see in the distance is the realization of My character, My Glory, towards which with varying pace you are hourly progressing.

The way to secure better progress is to keep your gaze on your goal. Not on the road you traverse, assuredly not on the way by which you have come. Your goal is that Glory or Character that you see more and more clearly in Me, your Lord and Master.

"It doth not yet appear what you shall be, but know that when I shall appear (that is to you, to your sight, when you see Me), you shall be like Me, for you shall see Me as I *am*."

JUNE

Confidence   June 1

CHARACTER-CHANGE comes by doing My Will in days when you see no Vision and hear no Voice.

Never leave the path of strict observance of all you were told to do when you saw Me and spoke to Me on the Mount. If you do you walk into serious danger.

These dull days are your practice days. Difficulties appear, failure seems inevitable. But all is necessary, so that you may learn to adapt your life to the teaching I have given you, may realize your own weakness, develop obedience and perseverance, without waiting for further instruction and inspiration.

Persevere with patience. I guide you still, for I am with you when you do not realize My Presence.

More faith will come through the confidence arising from experience.

Shake Free   June 2

Come unto Me . . . and I will give you rest.

REST in the midst of work. Heart-rest in the knowledge of My keeping Power.

Feel that rest stealing into your being. Incline your ear and come unto Me, hear and your soul shall live. Grow in strength, not overgrown by cares.

Let not the difficulties of life, like weeds, choke the rest of your soul, choke and tether the soaring freedom of your spirit.

Rise above these earth-bonds into newness of life, abundant and victorious. Rise.

Praise for Everything   June 3

CONFIDENCE must be the finishing chord of every contact between you and Me. Joyful confidence. You must end upon the Joy-note.

The union between a soul and Me is attained in its beauty and complete satisfaction only when in every incident that soul achieves praise.

Love and laugh and thank Me all the time.

Delve   June 4

CONSIDER the Truths of My Kingdom as well worth all search, all sacrifice. Dig down into the soil. Dig when it means toil, fatigue.

Above and below the ever-present material you must look for My Hidden Treasure. It is not what you say, but what you perceive, that will influence other lives.

My Spirit will communicate this to you and also to those round you. So for their sakes delve.

Delve Further   June 5

EXAMINE yourself. Ask Me and I will show you what you are doing wrong—if only you will listen humbly and be unreservedly determined to do My Will.

True Joys   June 6

CONTINUE ye in My Love. Seek nothing for yourself, only what you can use for Me. Rely on Me for all. Be meek, not only towards Me but towards others. Love to serve. Have no fear. Seek to be true in all. Be full of Joy.

The world wants to see Joy, not in the thrills of worldly pleasures and dissipations, but in the beauty of Holiness. In the ecstasy of peaceful safety with Me. In that thrill of adventure My true followers know, in the satisfaction that self-conquest gives.

Let your world see that you are steadfast, immovable.

Lose Life's Sting   June 7

SUBMIT yourself entirely to My Control, My Kingship; then the sting is taken out of life's rebuffs.

Welcome each contact as of My planning. Be ready to widen your circle of influence at My wish. Do not let age or other limitations daunt you.

Trust Me. Can I not judge your fitness for the task I give you? Have not I a Love for your acquaintances as well as for you?

Do not question My decisions. All is planned in Love for all My children. Only self-will can hinder the carrying out of the Divinely-conceived plan.

Work gladly, knowing all needed wisdom shall be provided, also all needed material to do My Work.

Perennial Youth   June 8

COUNT all well lost, all other work well foregone, to rest apart with Me.

From these times you go out strengthened, glad, full of Life-giving Joy—My Joy that you can never find anywhere else but with Me, the Joy-giving Christ.

Let others sense this Joy. More than any words this will show them the priceless gain of life with Me.

You shall truly find that there is no age in My Kingdom, in My Companionship.

Set Apart   June 9

COUNT not these days as lost.

You have, even in this seemingly narrow life, countless opportunities for self-conquest. There is no greater task than that.

I set apart those who greatly desire to reflect Me, because there is danger that in the crowded ways, and among others, self will gain the ascendancy.

For a time, until self is recognized and conquered, you too must withdraw into the wilderness.

You are learning much, and I am your Teacher.

Come with Me into a desert place and rest awhile.

Do You Remember? June 10

CULTIVATE the habit of thinking about Me. God is everywhere. My Presence is always with you, but recollection brings consciousness of that Presence and closer friendship.

Deliberately recall some event in My life, some teaching of Mine, some act of love. So will you impress Me upon your character and life.

Your learning and accomplishments are valueless without My Grace, which is sufficient for you. Leave planning to Me. Leave Me to open or close the way.

Prepare yourself for all I am preparing for you.

Simple Obedience June 11

Dear Lord, teach me to obey Thee in all things.

You are Mine, pledged to serve Me.

Every want of yours has been anticipated. Look back and see how each failure has been due to your not having obeyed implicitly the instructions I gave you in preparation for that task or trial.

Listening to My Voice implies obedience. I am a tender Lord of Love, but I am a Captain with whose words there must be no trifling.

You are a volunteer, no conscript, but if you expect the privileges of My Service you must render Me the obedience of that service.

The way of obedience may seem hard and dreary, but the security of My ordered life the untrained soul can never know. March in step with your Captain.

Spiritual Renewal   June 12

DEEP life-giving draughts of My Spirit are yours.

Think of the aridness, the thirst, that is unquenched till the whole unsatisfied being is age-worn.

Can you help man in any better way than by proving to him that the cleansing waters of My Spirit have power to wash away all that hinders growth, and to satisfy to the full every thirst of your nature.

Conquest of Fear   June 13

IT is not thinking about Me, but dwelling with Me that brings perfect fearlessness.

There can be no fear where I am. Fear was conquered when I conquered all Satanic power. If all My followers knew this, and affirmed it with absolute conviction, there would be no need of armed forces to combat evil.

The Soul Restored   June 14

Do not sorrow if, after time with Me, you cannot repeat to yourself all the lessons you have learned. Enough that you have been with Me.

Do you need to know the history of plant or tree to enjoy the countryside? You have inhaled pure air and been refreshed with the beauty of the landscape. Enough for the day. So, too, you have been in My Presence and found rest unto your souls.

Down in the Valley   June 15

Do not let doubt or fear assail or depress you because of this time of anguish and failure-sense through which you have passed. No, this had to be.

Useful work lies ahead of you. Before the onset of so great a task My servant has usually to walk through the Valley of Humiliation, or in the wilderness.

If I, your Lord, before I began My Mission, had to have My forty days of temptation, how could you expect to go all unprepared to your great task?

You must taste anew the shame of unworthiness, of failure and of nothingness before you go forth with Me conquering and to conquer.

Down into Egypt   June 16

Down into Egypt, back into Galilee. These journeys were gladly undertaken. They meant no family upheaval, for was not the desire of that Family but to fulfil Divine Intent?

Upheavals come only when man is set on some particular way of life, and is called to forgo that.

When the fixed desire is to do the Father's Will, then there is no real change. The leaving of home, town, country is but as the putting off of a garment that has served it useful purpose.

Change is only Spiritual progress when the life is lived with Me, the Changeless One.

Bind Their Wounds   June 17

DRAW from Me not only the Strength you need for yourself, but all you need for the wounded ones to whom I shall lead you. Remember no man liveth to himself. You must have Strength for others.

They will come to you in ever-increasing numbers. Will you send them empty away? Draw from Me and you will not fail them.

Nearer to Thee   June 18

"LORD, show me Thyself," is a cry that never goes unanswered.

Not often to physical vision comes the awareness but to spiritual insight, as more and more you realize My Love, My Power, and the manifold wonders of My character—its humility, its Majesty, its tenderness, its sternness, justice, mercy, healing and consuming fire.

Draw nigh to Me and I will draw nigh to you.

My Healing Power   June 19

WHEN life is difficult then relax completely; sleep or rest in conscious reliance on My Healing Power.

Endeavour that others may never see you anything but rested, strong, happy, joyful.

Before you meet seek renewal in My Secret Place.

Your tears and cares must be shared with Me alone.

My blessing be upon you.

Living Waters   June 20

DRINK of the water that I shall give you, and you shall never thirst.

I will lead you beside the waters of comfort.

I will give unto you living water.

Blessed are they that hunger and thirst after righteousness.

As the hart panteth after the water brooks so longeth my soul after Thee, O God.

This is the thirst that can never go unsatisfied.

Yours   June 21

APPEAL to Me often. Do not *implore* so much as *claim* My Help as your right.

It is yours in Friendship's name. Claim it with a mighty, impelling insistence. It is yours.

Not so much Mine to give you, as yours; but yours because it is included in the Great Gift of Myself that I gave you.

An All-embracing Gift, a Wonder Gift. Claim, accept, use it. All is well.

Right of Entry   June 22

DWELL with Me, and in doing so you admit those you love to the right of entry.

If their thoughts follow you as human friend

and helper, they are drawn in thought, and later in love and longing, to Me with whom you live.

Each Need Supplied   June 23

INSTEAD of urging men to accept Me as this or that, first discover the need, and then represent Me as the supply.

A man may not feel his need of a Saviour. He wants a Friend. Reveal Me as the Great Friend. Another may not need guidance, only to be understood. Represent Me as the Understanding Christ.

Leave Me to satisfy each and every need as I do yours.

Zest in Service   June 24

YOUR will, your desire, must be to do My Will, wanting It, loving It, as a child hugging some treasure to its heart. So treasure My Will.

Find your delight in It. "Lord, what would'st Thou have me to do?" is no question of a sullen servant. It is the eager appeal of a friend, who views all life as a glorious adventure, with the enthusiasm of a youth permitted to share an explorer's quest.

Bring the unquenchable Zest into all you do.

Ladder of Joy   June 25

YOU see in your lives cause for praise or prayer. You praise or pray. Your heart is lifted thereby into the Eternal, into My very Presence.

Thereafter the drudgery or commonplace or

dreary waiting ceases to be the colourless some-thing to be endured. It is the ladder, whereby you rise to Me.

You can then smile at it, welcome it. It is friend, not foe. So with everything in life. Its value for you must depend on whether it leads you nearer to Me.

So poverty or plenty, sickness or health, friend-ship or loneliness, sunshine or gloom, each may add to the Joy and Beauty of your lives.

Life's Furnace   June 26

LIFE has its furnace for My children, into which they are plunged for the moulding.

At their request I watch and watch until I can see them reflect My Glory. Then comes the fur-ther shaping into My Likeness. But the metal from which that Likeness is fashioned must be indeed pure.

So often My children are impatient for the moulding, never thinking that the refining must come first.

To do My work there must be much refining.

Eternal Life   June 27

ETERNAL Life is a matter of VISION.

Spiritual Vision is the result of knowledge which engenders further knowledge.

"And this is Life Eternal . . . to know Thee the only True God and Jesus Christ Whom Thou has sent."

Eternal Life.

Eternal in so far as the quality, the character of the Life is concerned. Being of God it implies immortality.

It is My Gift of the Life that is Mine. Therefore it must be Power-Life. This is your Life, to absorb, to live in, and through.

"He that believeth—*hath* eternal life."

The Life Divine   June 28

As you recognize My dealings with you, Eternal Life flows through your being in all Its sanctifying, invigorating and remedial force.

Eternal Life is awareness of the things of Eternity. Awareness of My Father and awareness of Me. Not merely a knowledge of Our existence, even of our God-head, but an awareness of Us in all.

As you become aware of Me, all for whom you care are linked to Me, too. Yielding Me your service, you draw, by the magnetic power of Love, all your dear ones within the Divine-Life radius.

All One   June 29

EVERY man is your brother, every woman your sister, every child your child. You are to know no difference of race, colour or creed. One is your Father and all ye are brethren.

This is the Unity I came to teach—Man united with God and His great family. Not man alone, seeking a oneness with God alone. See God the Father with His great world family, and, as you seek union with Him, it must mean for you attachment to His family, His other children.

He acknowledges all as His children, not all acknowledge Him as their Father.

Ponder this.

Immune from Evil   June 30

EVIL was conquered by Me, and to all who rely on Me there is immunity from it.

Turn evil aside with the darts I provide.

Rejoicing in tribulation is one dart.

Practising My Presence is another.

Self-emptying is another.

Claiming My Power over temptation is another.

You will find many of these darts as you tread My Way, and you will learn to use them adroitly, swiftly. Each is adapted to the need of the moment.

JULY

Out of the Unseen

> *Faith is the substance of things hoped for, the evidence of things not seen.*

You do not yet see, nor will you see fully while you are on this earth, how faith, co-operating with Spiritual Power, actually calls into being that for which you hope.

Men speak of dreams come true. But you know them as answered prayers; manifestations of Spirit Force in the Unseen. So trust boundlessly.

Dangerous Power

Do you not see how necessary is your learning the method of Spirit-attack. There must be a certain root-faith in Me, or you could not trust yourself to perfect surrender to Me. But there must come to those who walk all the way with Me, a yielding of their wills and lives wholly to Me, or the greater faith that results would be a source of danger. It would drag you back to the material plane, instead of to Spiritual Heights.

For unless your will is *wholly* Mine, you will rely on this new God-given Power, and call into being that which is not for the furtherance of My Kingdom.

Hiding in Thee

FOLLOW Me, and whether it be in the storm, or along the dusty highroad, or over the places of stones, or in the cool glade or the meadow, or by the waters of comfort, then, with Me, in each experience there will be a place of refuge.

At times you seem to follow afar off. Then weary with the burden and the way, you stretch out a hand to touch the hem of My Garment.

Suddenly there is no dust, no weariness. You have found Me. My child, even if it seems unprofitable, continue your drudgery, whether it be of spiritual, mental or physical effort. Truly it serves its turn if it but lead you to seek help from Me.

Break Free

For by whom a man is overcome . . .
he is the slave.

I CUT the bonds of sin which bound you to evil. With loving Hands I replaced each with my cords of Love, which bound you to Me, your Lord.

The power of evil is subtle. A cut cord, a snapped cord, would awaken your slumbering conscience, but strand by strand, so carefully, with gentleness cunningly acquired, evil works until a cord is free. Even then the work is slow, but oh, so sure, until presently the old bond I severed is binding you to evil, strand by strand.

Snap off these returning fetters. Satan hath desired to have you that he may sift you as wheat. He works with an efficiency My servants would do well to copy. He has marked you as one who will increasingly bring souls to Me.

My Family Circle   July 5

For whosoever shall do the Will of My Father, he is My brother and sister and mother.

You see how everything depends on the necessity of doing the Will of My Father.

Here is the intimacy of a new relationship. The only condition of this is the doing of My Father's Will. Then at once, into the inner Family Circle there is admission.

The plain way of discipline is the way of knowing My Will. That is the first requisite to the doing of it.

My Will for each day can only be revealed as each day comes, and until one revelation has been lived out, how can you expect to be made aware of the next?

Awareness of My Will is only achieved by obedience to that Will as it is made clear, and when THAT Will has been obeyed the veil, hiding My next desire, is lifted.

Listen Carefully   July 6

My poor deaf world. What it misses in loving Words and Whispers.

I want to share so much with it. It will not listen.

"Wherefor do you spend money for that which is not bread and your labour for that which satisfieth not. Hearken diligently unto Me and eat that which is good and let your Soul delight itself . . ."

"He that willeth to do My Will—shall know."

Whose Voice would you hear? So many voices are about you that you may miss the Still Small Voice.

"This is My Beloved Son—Hear Him."

Love's Growth   July 7

Learn from Nature the profusion of her gifts.

As you daily realize more and more the generosity of the Divine Giver, learn increasingly to give.

Love grows by giving.

You cannot give bountifully without being filled with a sense of giving yourself with the gift, and you cannot so give without Love passing from you to the one who receives.

You are conscious, not of yourself as generous, but of the Divine Giver as bounteous beyond all human words to express.

So Love flows *into* you with an intensity that is both humbling and exalting as Love flows *from* you with your gift.

Remember Me   July 8

> *Give me a constant remembrance of Thee.*

Ask what you will and it shall be done unto you. But only if the heart desires what the lips express. "The Lord looketh on the heart."

You will grow into the true attitude of remembrance of Me as you learn more and more to attribute all your blessings, all your guidance, to My increasing care: to the mind of your Master behind all, inspiring all, controlling all, the source of all your good.

Upheld   July 9

Go forward unafraid.

Face each difficulty, however great and seemingly unconquerable, as you go forward towards it.

The strength you will require from Me for that adventure into danger, as it may seem to you, will fortify you for its overcoming.

"Fear thou not, for I am with thee,

"Be not afraid for I am thy God.

"I will strengthen thee, I will help thee,

"Yea, I will uphold thee with the right arm of My Righteousness."

Your Heart Is Fixed   July 10

STILL go forward unafraid. The way will open as you go.

It is fear that blocks My way for you. Have no fear. Know that all is well.

No circumstances, no outward changes, can harm you in any way. Each should prove a step of progress, as long as your hearts are fixed "trusting in the Lord."

I know no change.

Go on in faith and trust. The Way opens as you go. In the Christian Life doors swing open as you come to them, if so be that you have advanced to them along the straight path of obedience.

As you started your journey, what would it have profited had you worried about the closed door ahead?

In the Spirit-Life miracle-working Power operates through natural human channels. As you have seen.

So this is the continuing lesson: Go steadily forward in firm trust along the path of quiet obedience.

That is *your* work. *Mine* to cause the doors to swing open, as you come to them, not before.

How often have I opened those doors for you in the past? More will open. So trust, so hope, so love.

Your Order of Merit   **July 12**

GRACE is the distinctive mark I set upon My friends.

It is no order of merit. It is the result of living with Me. It is even unobserved by those on whom I bestow it, but to those they meet who have eyes to see, it is apparent, just as during My time on earth it was said, "They took knowledge of them that they had been with Jesus."

It may be the sign of My sustaining Power within a life. It may be the quiet strength of poise, the mark of self-conquest, some faint reflection of My character, or a mystic scent of the soul unfolding to My Love.

Harmonize   July 13
GROW daily, ever more and more, into My likeness

Do My Will as revealed to you, and leave the result to Me. If you are but My representative, then why concern yourself as to whether the action I have arranged for you is wise or not?

If your control of mind and body is not as progressive as that of your spirit, it is a hindrance. See to this. The three must work in unison; otherwise disharmony.

Beautiful though one instrument may be in an orchestra, with a beauty beyond that of any other, yet should it play its part ahead of those others, disharmony results; and so with you a sense of frustration and failure follows disharmony within.

Home of Creation   July 14
HAVE no fear. Wonders are unfolding ever more and more. You will be guided in all as you dwell in the Secret Place of the Most High.

Remember in that Secret Place was thought out all the wonders of the Universe. There all *your* wonder plans will be evolved. It is the home of Creation, and there you, too, share in Creative Power.

HEART speaks to heart as you wait before Me. Love enkindles Love.

The air you breathe is Divine, life-giving, invigorating.

The place in which you rest is My Secret Place. You do not come to ask Me of doctrine.

That is, as it were, the foundation of your Spiritual being; necessary but once secure, you seek to fashion, with Me, its beautiful superstructure —the home of Peace and Joy where I come and commune with you.

Confidences   July 16

HELP is always yours.

It comes so swiftly when you realize that *you* are insufficient to supply your need. But it comes the more potently as you grow to see that for each need the supply was already provided.

My followers so often act as if My supply came into being only through prayer for help.

Would any man in authority act thus in his business?

Learn of Me. I will teach you lovingly, patiently. My lessons are not of the schoolroom; they are fireside confidences.

Foretaste of Heaven   July 17

I thank Thee, Lord, for the Joy Thou givest me and for Thy tender care of me.

GROW ever more and more conscious of this. Look

upon all as under My Influence, and life will become increasingly full of Joy. This Joy no man taketh from you.

This is the foretaste of Heaven that will make your passing seem no death, and will mean that your spirit will be no stranger in the home of spirits but will be breathing an atmosphere familiar and dear.

Meek and Lowly   July 18

As the world's great Teacher I taught not so much by word as by the Living Word.

"Learn of Me" I said, adding that men should see in Me meekness . . . and lowliness.

So that My disciples should take Me as their great example, I epitomised My attitude towards My Father in Heaven and towards His other children as "Meek and lowly."

Towards God the Father the meekness of a yielded will; towards His other children lowliness devoid of the pride that sunders men and prevents their humble approach to God.

"Learn of Me—I am meek and lowly in heart." So do you find rest unto your souls.

Wayside Meetings   July 19

I USE such simple things and casual moments to reveal Myself to man. He can meet Me in the common ways of Life—if he has but eyes to see and ears to hear.

No great sign, nothing spectacular. In the seemingly incidental along the road of life I meet with him and reveal My Will, My Purpose, My Guidance.

No miles to walk, no long journey to travel, no strange language to learn, no state of ecstasy to be experienced first. Think on these things. Recall our many meetings by the wayside.

I Will Heal You   July 20

Do not recognize your illness. Each time you speak of it to others you stabilize it.

Ignore it as much as you can. Think more of Me, the Great Healer. Dwelling with Me you become whole.

Even My most faithful followers often err in not claiming of Me healing and perfection for every part of their being.

But to claim physical healing alone is a sign of living too much on the physical plane, and My Healing is of the Spirit.

Claim healing of spirit, mind and body. Then shall you, regardless of age, know wholeness.

Unconquerable   July 21

I WILL help you to conquer in the hour of temptation or difficulty. Cling to Me. Rest in My Love. Know that all is well.

Trials press, temptations assail, but remember, you can be more than conquerors through Me. Lord of all, I am. Controller of all. Keeper, Lover, Guide, Friend.

Remember that when once your hearts have said with Peter, "Thou art the Christ, the Son of the Living God," then upon that sure foundation of relief I raise My House, My Holy of Holies.

The gates of hell, the adverse deeds and thoughts and criticisms of the world, cannot prevail against it. More than conquerors. Conquer in the little things. Conquer in My Strength and Power.

Lend a Hand   July 22

NOT once only in your lives, when I called you out to follow Me, but constantly—

Jesus calls.

In the busy day, in the crowded way, listen to the voice of your Lord and Lover calling. A call to stop and rest with Me awhile. A call to restrain your impatience, a reminder that in quietness and in confidence shall be your strength. A call to pause, to speak a word to one in trouble.

Perhaps to lend a hand.

Dear Name   July 23

THE murmuring of My Name in tender Love brings the unseen into the foreground of reality. It is like breathing on some surface, which brings into relief a lovely figure.

It is the Name before which evil shrinks away, shamed, powerless, defeated. Breathe it often. Not always in appeal. Sometimes in tender confidence, sometimes in Love's consciousness. Sometimes in triumphant ecstasy.

Christian Co-operators   July 24

I HAVE always work to be done. So fit yourself for

it by prayer, by contact with Me, by discipline.

Nothing is small in My sight. A simple task fittingly done may be the necessary unit in building a mighty edifice.

The bee knows nothing of its agency when fertilizing flowers for fruit-bearing.

Do not expect to see results.

The work may pass into other hands before any achievement is apparent. Enough that you are a worker with others and Me in My Vineyard.

Joy in Me   July 25

Joy teaches. Joy cleans the smeared glass of your consciousness, and you see clearly.

You see Me clearly, and see more clearly the needs of those round you.

Perfect Yourself   July 26

PERFECT as My Father in Heaven is perfect.

That means a life-struggle, an unending growth. Always as you progress, a greater perception of My Father. More struggles and growth. Above all a growing need of Me and My sustaining help.

I came to found a Kingdom of Progressive growth. Alas, how many of My followers think that all they have to do is to accept Me as Saviour. That is a first step only.

Heaven itself is no place of stagnation. It is indeed a place of progress. You will need Eternity to understand Eternal Mind.

Judge Not July 27

HUMAN nature is so complex. You can hardly, even in your most enlightened moments, tell what motive prompted this or that action of your own.

How, then, can you judge of another, of whose nature you have so little understanding? And to misjudge of what in another may have been prompted by the Spirit of God, is to misjudge God's Spirit.

Can any sin be greater than that? False judgment sent Me to the Cross!

Stupendous Truth July 28

THE world can be overcome only by belief in Me, and in the knowledge that I am the Son of God. This is a stupendous Truth.

Use that as your lever for removing every mountain of difficulty and evil. Be cautious in all things and await My Guidance. Commune much with Me.

The truth of My God-head, of My All-Power, creative, redemptive, erosive of evil, must permeate your whole consciousness, and affect your attitude in every situation, toward every problem.

See the Lovable July 29

Do not try to force yourself to love others. Come to Me. Learn to love Me more and more, to know Me more, and little by little you will see your fellowman as I see him. Then you, too, will love him.

Not only with the Love of Me, which makes

you desire to serve him, but you will see the lovable in him, and love that.

Real Influence   July 30

Do not let one single link of influence go.

Cords of true love and interest must never be broken. They must always be used for ME. Pray for those to whom you are bound by particular ties, then you will be ready, should I desire your special help for them.

You must stand as a sinner with a sinner before you can save him. Even I had to hang between two thieves to save My world.

All in Order   July 31

He ordered my goings.

GUIDANCE first, but more than that, Divine order in your life, your home, all your affairs.

Order in all. Attain spiritual order first. The perfect calm which can be realized only by a soul that abides in My Secret Place.

Then the mental order of a mind which is stayed on Me and has the sanity and poise of a mind so stayed.

Then truly must order manifest itself in your surroundings.

Each task will be entered upon with prayer, as a Divine Commission, and carried through without haste, in utter contentment.

AUGUST

Joy of Harvest

He that reapeth receiveth wages and gathereth fruit unto life everlasting, that both he that reapeth and he that soweth may rejoice together.

Do you not see that if you are careless about the reaping you have prevented the harvest-joy of the sower?

If by your life and character you do not reap to the full that which they have sown, you are robbing them of the well-earned fruit of their labours.

Further learn this lesson. There are many of My workers and servants in different spheres of activity to whom you owe the seed of word or example or loving help that has influenced you.

It is a sacred trust. Use it fully.

Still Love and Laugh

THIS has ever been My command to you. Love and Laugh. There is a quality about true Love to which laughter is attune.

The Love that does not pulse with joy (of which laughter is the outward sign) is but solicitude. The Joy of Heaven is consciousness of God's Love.

It was that Love that brought Me to your world.

Consciousness of that Love called forth your joy. Study My Words in the Upper Room—

"Loved of My Father"; "I will love him"; "That your Joy might be full."

Love Lightens the Load   August 3

In due season you shall reap if you faint not.

THE way may seem long and dreary.

Sometimes My Heart of Love aches that I have to ask you to tread so long and so weary a way. Yet to each of My followers the road chosen is surely the one best suited to his feet.

But feet grow weary. Have you let Love smooth the toilsome way? We walk together.

Vision of Love   August 4

LOVE is the flower.

Love is the seed from which that flower germinates.

Love is the soil in which it is nourished and grows.

Love is the sun that draws it to fulfilment.

Love is the fragrance that flower gives out.

Love is the vision that sees its beauty, *and*

God is Love, all-knowing, all-understanding, from whom all Good proceeds.

Love in the Unlovely   August 5

LOVE to all must mark all you do if you own Me Lord, and if you would be a true follower of Me.

"His banner over me was Love." Those words express not only the loving Protection round you, but the banner under which you march as soldiers of Me, your Captain.

It serves to remind you of that for which you stand before the world. It is in Love's Name you march. In Love's Name you conquer. It is Love you are to take into the unlovely places of the world. It is the only equipment you need.

Deaf Ears   August 6

MAN cries for help. Man feels his need of Me. All unmindful that countless times I draw near unheard, pass on unnoticed, speak to deaf ears, touch brows fretted and wrinkled by earth's cares.

"The Christ is dead," man says.

Alive and longing, full of a living tenderness I passed his way to-day. He heeded not.

Man hears the storms, the wind, the earthquake, and his ears still pulsing with the echoes he hears no Still Small Voice. Oh, do not miss Me, My children.

Balm for All Ills   August 7

LOVE and care and pray. Never feel helpless to aid those you love. I am their help. As you obey Me and follow My teaching in your daily life, you will bring that help into operation.

So, if you desire to be used to save another, turn to your own life. As far as you can, make it all that it should be.

Let your influence for Me extend ever further and further. Let Love be your balm for all ills.

The Power in which you will break down all barriers.

It stands, too, for the Name of the God you love and serve. So with His banner floating o'er you, go on in glad confidence to victory. Your task to help, to strengthen, raise, heal. Only as you love will you do this.

No Hurt   August 8

He that overcometh shall not be hurt
by the second death.

THE first death is the death to self, the result of overcoming, of self-conquest. This is gradual death.

When it is complete, the second death shall cause no hurt. For it is only the conquering Spirit sloughing away its human habitation for a better Life.

The courage My Martyrs showed was not only fearlessness engendered in time of persecution through faith in Me, and in My power to support and sustain. It was consequent on the overcoming of self already achieved. Self, having truly died, this second death had no hurt for them.

Theirs was then the Risen Life with Me.

Undivided   August 9

LIVE in My Peace.

There must be no divided life in this.

Peace in your heart. That heart-rest that comes from constant communion with Me, and from an undisturbed trust in Me.

Then Peace round you, where others are conscious of Me, and of that Peace as My Gift, and the rest and strength and charm into which they are drawn.

Glad Surprise   August 10

LIVE so near to Me that you may never miss the opportunity of being used by Me. It is the prepared instrument, lying nearest to the Master Craftsman's Hand, that is seized to do the work.

So be very near Me, and you cannot fail to be much used. Remember that Love is the Great Interpreter, so that those who love you and are near to you are the ones you can help the most.

Do not pass them by for others, though your influence and helpfulness will gradually spread, in an ever-widening circle. You will live in a spirit of glad surprise.

Absolute Honesty   August 11

LEARN to act slowly with sanctified caution.

Precipitancy has no part in My Kingdom.

Be more deliberate in everything, with the deliberation that should characterize every soul, for it is one of the credentials of that Kingdom.

Lack of poise and dignity means lack of Spiritual Power, and this it must be your aim to possess.

Be truthful in all things, honest with an honesty that can be challenged by the world, and by the standards of My Kingdom, too.

Holy Revelry

LIVE with Me. Work with Me. Ever delight to do *My Holy Will*. Let *this* be the satisfaction of your lives. Revel in it.

Let the wonder of My care for you be so comforting that you may see no dullness in drudgery, in delay . . .

The Glory of My leading, the wonder of its intimacy reveals such tender knowledge of you, past and future.

Let this reveal Me to you, and so daily increase your knowledge of Me.

The Road You Took

LOOK back at the way I have led you.

Say to yourself, "Is not my Lord as strong today as in the days that lie behind me? Did He not save me when human aid was powerless? Did He not keep His Promise, and protect and care for me? Can I, remembering that, doubt His Power now?"

So you will gain confidence and a firmer trust. As your faith is thus strengthened My Power can operate more freely and fully on your behalf.

You are only beginning to realize My Wonders. You will see them unfold more and more as you go on. Bring Me into all you do, into every plan, every action.

Riches of His Grace

IT is for My followers to make My Word, the

very Word of God, attractive.

My Word has to *dwell* in you richly. There must be no stinting, no poverty, but an abundance of rich supply.

Note the *dwell*. Nothing fitful, as I have told you. Make its home there. Fittingly belong there. No question of meagre or exhausted supply.

The Word of God grows in meaning, in intensity, for you, as you bring it into operation.

Remember, too, the Word of God is that Word made flesh, Who dwells with you, your Lord Jesus Christ.

My Image Restored   August 15

Look unto Me until your gaze becomes so intense that you absorb the Beauty of Holiness.

Then truly is the petty, unworthy self ousted from your nature. Look to Me. Speak to Me. Think of Me.

So you become transformed by the renewing of your mind. Other thoughts, other desires, other ways follow, for you become transformed into My Likeness.

Thus you vindicate the ways of God with man —man made in His image, that Image marred, but I still had trust in man; trust that man, seeing the God-Image in Me, the man Christ Jesus, would aspire to rise again—into My Likeness.

Expectancy   August 16

In all your work, your meetings with others, have ever the consciousness of My brooding Love surrounding you. Continue ye in My Love.

Meet Me at eventide with loving expectancy.

Premature Blessing   August 17

Give me strength to wait Thy time, accept Thy discipline.

ONLY your failure to do this can delay the answers to your many prayers.

The blessing you crave needs a trained, disciplined life, or it would work your ruin and bring upon you a world's criticism that could but harm the very cause, My cause, which you so ardently seek to serve.

Broken Bonds   August 18

Loose the fetters that bind me to earth and material things.

THEY shall be loosed. Even now your prayer is being answered. But you can only be completely released as you live with Me more and more.

Thought-freedom from self-claims comes by a process of substitution. For every claim of self, substitute My claim. For every thought of fear or resentment substitute a thought of security in Me and of Joy in My Service. For every thought of limitation, of helplessness, substitute one of the Power of a Spirit-aided life.

Do this persistently. At first with deliberate effort, until it becomes an almost unconscious habit. The fetters will snap and gradually you will realize the wonder of your freedom.

Bounteous Giving August 19

Lord I ask for Thine unlimited supply.

I GIVE with no niggard hand. See the Beauty in Nature, the profusion, the generosity. When I give you a work to do, a need of another's to meet, My supply knows no bounds.

You, too, must learn this Divine generosity, not only towards the lonely, the needy, whom you contact, but towards Me, your Lord.

Measure the wealth of Mary's gift by the offerings given to Me nowadays by those who profess their Love for Me. Ungenerous giving dwarfs the soul.

Glorious Opportunity August 20

MAN's life is no tragedy or comedy staged by a God of Whims.

It is man's glorious opportunity of regaining what humanity lost—assisted by the One Who found the path-direct, and Who is ready at every point, and all along the way to supply man with the Life Eternal.

That Life Eternal which alone enables him to breathe, even here and now, the very air of Heaven, and to be inspired with the Spirit-Life in which I lived on earth; God made man.

Where to Find Me—Always August 21

MAN so often seeks and marvels that he does not find. Why? Because only along the path of simple obedience am I to be found.

I said, "I came not to do Mine own Will but the Will of Him that sent Me." I tread, as I always trod, the path of simple obedience. Along it shall I be found.

Man must be simply obedient to My Commands before his feet can come My way. Then, seeking, he truly finds Me. I said you must become as little children to enter the Kingdom of Heaven.

True Power   August 22

MANY are speaking ABOUT Me, and they marvel that their words have no force. They are not My Words, they are words about Me. Oh, how different.

The world is surfeited with words about Me.

The world needs to *see Me, not to hear of My Power, but to see it in action.* Not to hear of My Peace, but to see that it keeps My followers calm, unruffled and untroubled, no matter what the outward circumstances.

Not to *hear* of My Joy, but to *see* it, as from hidden depths of security, where true Power and Peace abide, it ripples to the surface of the life, and is revealed to those round about.

Hunger for Righteousness   August 23

MANY are wondering why their desire for righteousness is not satisfied according to My Promise. But that Promise was on condition that there should be hunger and thirst. If the Truths I have given have not been absorbed, there can be no real hunger for more.

So, when you miss the Joy-Light on your path, when the vision seems lost, and the Voice silent, then ask yourself, have you failed to live out the lessons that you were taught?

Live out My teaching in your lives, and then, hungry for more, come to Me, Bread of Life, Food of your souls.

Might and Majesty   August 24

You see Me sometimes as the Man of Sorrows.

Behold Me, too, in the Majesty of My God-head.

Not always can man disregard My Wishes and break My Commands.

I view the desecration of My Image, I see the ruin of the kingdom of earth which was to have been the Kingdom of the Lord. I see passions let loose and innocence spoiled, and man clamouring for the mastery.

Then the Man of Sorrows walks a King with flashing eyes, as He sees the down-trodden, the oppressed, the persecuted and the persecutor, the tyrant and the weak.

How long shall I have the patience? HOW LONG?

House of the Spirit   August 25

"Lest perhaps you should let them slip"—"Hold fast that thou hast." Each Truth learned has to be cemented to your being by obedience.

Your soul-character is like a building. It IS a building (the Temple) in which the God-Spirit can make a Home.

Bricks lying on the ground separate are useless; placed together, united, they form a building. So obedience is the mortar by which Truths are retained and become a part of the being. Truths which would otherwise be lost.

So every Truth I give you must be lived out.

"I Die Daily" August 26

I ENJOINED that if any man would follow Me he should deny himself and take up his cross.

The denial thus impressed upon My disciples as necessary was not a mere matter of discipline, of giving up, of going without.

It was a total repudiation of any claim the self might make, ignoring it, refusing to acknowledge it.

Not *once* was this to be done, but *daily;* there was to be a daily recrucifixion of any part of the self-life not already completely dead.

One Spirit-led Family August 27

HAVE no fear. Wonders unfold.

In this Life or in the Larger Life, the lesson is the same—the absorption of My Spirit—living, thinking and acting in My Spirit until others are forced to see and recognize its Power and claims.

Does this mean loneliness for My Follower? Nay, rather, though you, the human-self-you has no recognition, the real you, transformed by My Spirit, shares in all that fulness of operation and resultant Joy.

You are no isolated being but one of a mighty Spirit-led family, partaker of all the family's well-being, co-operative in every act of each member, sharer of the blessing of each.

A foretaste this of Heaven's oneness and fulfilment.

Thread of Gold   August 28

LET My Spirit of Calm enter your being, and direct you, filling you with Peace and Power. Find in each day that thread of gold that runs through all, and that links up all the simple tasks and words and interests and feelings into one whole.

Consciously hand the day back to Me at its close, leaving with Me all that is incomplete. It is Heaven's work to complete man's imperfect or unfinished task, when it has been of Heaven's ordering.

See the Joy of Life, and you by that very act increase it. Joy grows by man's consciousness of Joy.

Divine Extravagance   August 29

Let Christ be in you in all wealth of Wisdom.

IT is the niggard attitude of My followers that casts a slur upon My religion.

Dwell upon the Divine extravagance of terms used by those who know something of the wonder of My Kingdom—"The riches," "The wealth," "The fulness." There is no stint with God.

The only limit is set by the inability of My followers to take. Wealth of wisdom and unlimited Power to help others may be yours.

Stand Invincible   August 30

LIFE, earth-life, is a battle. A battle in which man will always be the loser unless he summon Eternal Life-Forces to his aid. Do this and all that has the power to thwart you slinks back defeated.

Say, in the little as well as in the big things of life, "Nothing can harm, nothing can make me afraid. In Him I conquer." Stand invincible, face to the foes of life.

Heaven's Music   August 31

LIFT up your heart.

Lift it up—its love and its longings, leaving fears and faults behind.

Let your heart draw its strength and vitalising Joy and Confidence from Me, your Lord.

Let no vibration stir your being that is not in harmony with the Eternal Music of My Kingdom.

SEPTEMBER

It Is Enough

LISTEN and I will speak.

I seldom force an entrance through many voices and distracting thoughts. There must be first the coming apart and then the stilling of all else as you wait in My Presence. Is it not enough that you are with Me?

Let that sometimes suffice.

It is truly much that I *speak* to you. But unless My Indwelling Spirit is yours, how can you carry out My wishes and live as I would have you live?

You Shall Hear

LISTEN to My Voice. Share all your joys and sorrows and difficulties with Me, remembering always that we share the work.

More and more souls will be sent to you to help. Be ready, attuned to My slightest whisper. There is no lack of help for My servants, but so often they are not in a receptive mood.

Listen and you shall hear, is the continuation of "Ask, and you shall receive," "Seek, and ye shall find," "Knock, and it shall be opened unto you——"

Listen, and you shall hear.

Your Failures Are Mine September 3

Lord I present to Thee my failures.
Only Thou couldst . . . repair the harm
that I have wrought.

BECAUSE you are Mine I must identify Myself with all you are. I play the harmony of which you made such discord. I sound the hope in ears you had no charm of Love to woo from sin and failure.

I lead to happier ways those you misjudged, despised.

I take your failures, and because your desire is towards Me, and you know Me as Lord, these, your failures, it is My sacrificial task to bear, to reclaim.

Step up from your slough of failure in the robe of faith and love I give you.

Be strong to save as you have known salvation, strong in Me, your ever-conquering Lord.

We Walk Together September 4

Lord I would walk with Thee.

SEE, I set My pace to yours as a loving parent does to that of his child.

So there must be much silence in our companionship because you are not yet able to bear all the Wonder-Truth I long to impart.

But though words might find you unresponsive, you cannot fail to grow in My Presence, to grow in Grace, to grow in understanding.

So in that Rest I promised to those who come

to Me, you do indeed gain the strength that comes from security in Love.

Love Leaps Forward September 5

You must keep close to Me.

Faithfulness is not merely obeying the expressed commands of My Written Word. It is the intuitive knowing of My Wish by close and intimate contact, from which has grown true understanding of Me.

Even with this, knowing faithfulness can only be possible when you are fortified with the Strength that Communion with Me gives.

If you know My slightest wish and have absorbed from Me the Strength in which to carry it out, then Love leaps forward, responsive, rejoicing in the Lord.

No Pride September 6

ARE you ready for training and discipline? Like my winter-trees, seemingly useless and impotent to those who do not understand the enrooting in Me which keeps you steadfast amid storms and winter cold.

All through the dark months when your beauty (your power to help and shield) has been sacrificed, you are yet drawing in strength and sustenance.

The time to help will come again, and you will have learned to have no personal pride in the beauty of your foliage and the restfulness of your shade.

You will use them for those who need them, but will give the glory to Me, your Lord.

"Lord, My Lord!" September 7

THE human heart craves a Leader, one whose will it delights to obey.

It craves a oneness of aim and achievement with a loved one. It craves to be understood.

It craves to reveal itself without reservations and to gain only strength thereby.

To gain, too, an ever more intimate revelation of the heart of the loved one. Where can the heart of man find satisfaction as with Me?

Perfect Harmony September 8

No discordant note mars your intercourse with Me, for only with Me can life be perfect harmony.

There may be much to regret on your part, failure, disloyalty, fear, sin.

In My Holy Presence all that is swept away by My Hand of Love. Only Love, Peace-bringing, Harmony-producing Love remains. If you are to face the World and maintain your calm, you must take to the World, and your tasks in it My Peace and Harmony.

Thy Heart's Desires September 9

PAUSE upon the threshold of My House of plenty.

Pause in awe and in the joy of Worship.

He shall give thee thine heart's desires. Give your desires themselves, conceived as they are in union with the Divine Spirit, *and* receive their fulfilment.

Know this and let your heart sing with the joy of this Wonder of Supply.

Unruffled

PEACE. It is your task to keep this Peace in your hearts and lives. This is your work for Me. It is so all-important because if you lack it, then, as a channel, you are for the time useless.

Learn to sense the slightest ruffle on the surface of your lives. Learn to sense the smallest unrest in your heart-depths. Then back to Me until all is calm.

Think, some message may be undelivered because I cannot use you. Some tender word unspoken because self blocks your channel.

Only self can cause unrest, and My great Gift to My disciples was PEACE.

Lose This Desire

AGAIN I say, never judge another. That is one of My tasks I have never relegated to any follower.

Live with Me. So you will be enabled to see more of that inner self that I see in each one. Thus you will learn a humility that makes you lose desire to judge.

Oh, seek to love and understand all. Love them for My sake. They are Mine. As you live with Me you will see how I yearn over them, and long for them. Seeing this your love for Me must prevent your hurting Me by unkind criticism of those for whom I care.

Blame Not

NEVER seek to cast the blame on others.

If I bear your sins and those of others are you not casting your blame on Me?

If what is untoward is the result of your own fault or weakness, seek to remedy the cause by conquering the fault and overcoming the weakness.

If it has been caused by another, then apportion no blame, allow no thought of self to intrude to cause the slightest ruffle of your spirit-calm.

Safeguard the peace which I entrusted to you.

Cause of Sin

No longer has sin any power over you unless of your own deliberate choice.

The surest way to safeguard yourself against any temptation to sin is to learn to love to do My Will, and to love to have that Will done in all the little as well as in all the big things of your daily life.

So often man puzzles over this—If I have conquered sin, why is it then so powerful an enemy?

I conquered sin.

It has no power over any soul that does not want to sin. Then all that could lead to sin is desire.

I lay such stress on man's loving Me. If his love, his desire, is set on Me—he wills *only* to do My Will. Thus he is saved from sin.

Gifts for You

"NOT as the world giveth, give I unto you."

Not as the world giveth, but oh, infinitely more richly, more abundantly, give I unto you.

The world expects a return, or gives only in return. Not so do I. My only stipulation is receive!

But to receive My Power, My Gifts, you must have room for them, and full of self there is no room for Me and My Gifts.

So all I desire of you is to be emptied of self, and to desire Me.

Bold in Prayer   September 15

MY child, there is no arrogance in your assertion when you say, "I will not let Thee go unless Thou bless me."

Have not I ever told you to claim big things. In so doing you obey Me.

You do right to wrestle boldly in prayer. There are times for demanding, for claiming.

Now is the time to claim. You are in no doubt about My Will. Claim its manifestations on earth.

Adoration   September 16

NEVER forget to adore. That is the most beautiful form of prayer. It includes all others.

If you adore, it implies that trust in Me and love for Me without which all supplication fails to achieve its object. It implies thanksgiving, because adoration is born of repeated thanksgiving.

It also implies contrition.

Who could adore Me with a Joy-filled adoration, and not be conscious of unworthiness and of

My forgiveness and blessing? Adoration is Love-filled reverence.

Leave Him to Me   September 17

IN My Kingdom judgment is not man's role. There is one Judge, and even He reserves His judgment until the last chapter of man's life is written, until all the evidence is secured, so anxious is He to discover some extenuating circumstances, or to wait until by man's turning to Him and throwing himself upon His mercy, the position is altered, and the judge becomes the prisoner in the dock.

Then God the Father, knowing His Beloved Son accepts responsibility for the deed (has in fact already received the punishment Himself), is bound to pardon the human sinner.

You then in judging (poor, weak, foolish, contemptuous arrogance), are judging not the sinner but Me.

You Can Help   September 18

MY followers were to save My world—by keeping My Commands, by close union with Me, and by the indwelling Power of My Spirit.

But they were to be a peculiar people. My religion which was to change men's lives, and was to be so revolutionary as to separate families and re-organize governments, has become a convention, tolerated where not appreciated.

Its Truths have been modified to suit men's desires. Its followers carry no flaming sword, they bear no Message of a Love so tender as to heal every wound, so scorching as to burn out every evil. My Cross is out-dated, My Loving Father but the First Cause.

Man delights in his self-sufficiency, and seeks to persuade himself that all is well. Can he deceive a loving, understanding Father, who knows that under all the boasting there lurks fear, longings, despair?

Can I leave man so? Can I offer him Calvary, and if he will have none of it, leave him to his fate? I know too well his need of Me. "You can help Me."

Help Me   September 19

HELP Me to save your fellow-man as dear to Me as you are.

Do you not care that he should pass Me by? *¡Do you not care that he should pass Me by?*

Do you not care that he is lonely, hungry, desperate and far from the fold?

Led by the Spirit   September 20

LEARN to wait for spiritual Guidance until its suggestion is as clear to your consciousness as any command of officer to soldier, of master to servant. This recognition distinguishes My true follower from the many who call Me "Lord, Lord," and do not the things that I say.

There are many who live according to the Principles I laid down when on earth, but who do not act under the impulse of My Spirit day by day.

"For as many as are led by the Spirit of God, they are the sons of God."

Barriers Burned Away   September 21

My Light shall shine upon you. It shall illumine and cheer your way.

But it shall also penetrate the dark and secret places of your hearts revealing perhaps some unrecognized sin, fault or failing.

Desire its radiance not only for its comfort and guidance, but also for its revelation of all within you that is not wholly Mine.

I am the Sun of Righteousness. Rest in My Presence, not clamouring, not supplicating, but resting until the impurities of your being are burnt out, the dross of your character refined away, and you can go on strengthened and purified to do My work.

I Am Forgiveness   September 22

My Lord, forgive me I pray.

COULD I withhold forgiveness? I, who live ever to plead for My children, who told them that always when they pray they must forgive in their hearts?

I am God but I became man.

Perfect God and perfect man.

So human and yet so Divine.

Because I am Eternal—that I must *ever* be.

So see in Me all I enjoined My followers *they* must ever be and do. Could I withhold forgiveness?

Irritability Banished   September 23

CONSCIOUSNESS of My Presence imparts permanence and strength to all you do.

My Spirit permeating every part of your being, drives out all selfish irritability, while fortifying all the weak parts and attuning your being to Heaven's Music.

To think of Heaven as a place where you sing praises to Me is right, but the singing is with your whole being, as My pulsing Joy flows through it.

All on the Altar   September 24

ABSOLUTE Love must decide all your actions.

Fear nothing. Ride the storm.

Delight to do My Will.

Not only money affairs; lay all your letters, your work, all, upon My altar.

Make an offering of each day to Me for the answering of your prayers and for the salvation of My poor world.

Subdue every self-thought, utterly, entirely.

The Love That Satisfies   September 25

MY Mercies are great to all who turn to Me and to all who turn *from* Me.

How tenderly I yearn over these wayward ones. How I seek ever to save them from the hurts their very refusal of Me will bring upon them.

I long to save them from the hunger of lone-liness that will follow their driving away the only love that will satisfy.

Storms May Rage   September 26

LIVE with Me and words will not be necessary. You will know My Will.

The real necessity is your receptiveness.

That comes through self-discipline that allows of spiritual progress into, and in, a Higher Life.

In that spirit realm you are conscious of My Will. You are one with Me. Truly, you may count all things well lost to win Christ.

I wish you to learn the Glory of a God-protected, guided life. No idle, fruitless rushing hither and thither. Storms may rage, difficulties may press hard, but you will know no harm. Safe, protected and guided.

My Striving Spirit   September 27

THERE is never a time when a man cannot turn repentant to Me and, craving My pardon, receive it.

But there is a time when I cease to be persistent in urging My follower to an action.

The human ear can hear a sound so often until it ceases to convey a meaning, to be heard with awareness.

So with the spirit-ear, unless the whole desire and effort is to carry out My plan, My servant may cease to hear, cease to be aware of My wish.

This is a grave spiritual danger, and I say unto you, watch and guard against it.

Your Only Way   September 28

THERE is a stage in Christian development at which My follower should have passed beyond that of general service and conformity to the rules I laid down for My disciples.

When he should be seeking to serve in some special way planned for that soul, and in the service that soul was destined for, which none other can so adequately do.

Think, the Salvation of My world, all planned, even to the minutest detail, but that work is not done through neglect, through failure, through indifference.

My way for you is not a path of general righteousness and obedience, but the actual road mapped out for you, in which you can best help My needy world.

Love Heals   September 29

You are asking to be used by Me to heal, but you are asking for the fruit before the root has become established, and the tree has grown to its stature.

With the elimination of self, and obedience to My Will, your Power in the Spirit world will naturally grow. Thus you will assuredly gain in that world the control that others seek to have on the material plane.

But you must forego all desire for control or

recognition on that lower plane. As you cannot serve two masters, so neither can you operate on two planes.

Your Love must grow by dwelling with Me. It was My overflowing Love that healed.

The Future All Unknown   September 30

My Word shall be a lamp unto your feet, and a light unto your path. No difficulty need appal you. You shall know in all things what to do, but remember that the light must go with you. It is to warn, comfort and cheer, not to reveal the future.

My servants do not need to know that. The true child spirit rejoices in the present, and has no fears, no thought beyond it. So must you live.

If I, your Lord, accompany you, shedding My radiance all round you, the future must always be dark, because as far as your acceptance of revelation and your present development are concerned, I am not THERE.

But as the future of to-day becomes the present of to-morrow, then the same light and Guidance and Miracle-working Power will be yours. Rejoice evermore.

Have Confidence   October 1

NOTHING happens to you that is not the answer to your prayers, the fufilment of your desire to do, and have, in all, My Will.

So go forward into each day unafraid.

No Greater Joy   October 2

ON earth, or even in Heaven, there can be no greater joy than realizing that My Will is being accomplished in the little as well as in the big things.

Indeed, it can be *your* "meat" as I said it was *Mine*. It is the very sustenance of body, mind and spirit, that Trinity of being, symbolized in the Temple in the Outer Court, the Holy Place, and then in the very Holy of Holies, where man speaks with God and dwells with Him.

Into that Holy of Holies there can be no entrance except to sacrifice, to bring an offering of the physical and mental being in Spirit to identify the whole with that Supreme Sacrifice I offered for My World.

Constant Companion   October 3

Not unto us, O Lord . . . but unto Thy Name be Glory.

MY Name. I AM. Existent before all Worlds,

changeless through Eternity, changeless in Time.

All I have ever been through the ages I AM.

All that you ever crave I may be to you—I AM.

In a changing world you need to dwell much upon Me, your Master, the Jesus Christ of whom is was said—

"The same yesterday, to-day and for ever."

Then it follows that with you to-day is The Lord of Creation, the Jesus of Nazareth, the Christ of the Cross, the Risen Saviour, the Ascended Lord. What a Companionship for the uncertain ways of a changing world.

Bright Reality   October 4

O Jesus make Thyself to me
A living, bright reality.

THEN will you show Me as a living bright reality?

I died that I might live in you, My followers, and you present Me to the world as a dead Christ.

"I am alive for evermore."

Though you may repeat those words they are not vibrant with Life, here and now. They speak but of My existence in another sphere far removed from this earth and its joys and sorrows, achievement and stress.

Yet in all these daily things I would have My Spirit active in and through you.

How can man so misread My Teaching?

One with Me   October 5

ONE with the God of Creation.

One with the Jesus of Calvary.

One with the Risen Christ.

One with His Spirit operating in every corner of the Universe, energizing, renewing, controlling, all-powerful.

Could man ask more? Could thought rise higher?

Power-Seekers   October 6

How pitiful man's striving after power when God's Power, with all its mighty possibilities, is there for him did he but know how to obtain it.

To tell one such that this would only be possible for one who has entered My Kingdom of Heaven, might indeed arouse his curiosity.

But tell him the way into that Kingdom is one of self-effacement, obedience to and love of My Will, tell him that he must enter as a little child, that only by spiritual progress can he attain to man's true estate, and that the training might be long, the discipline hard—tell him this and he will turn empty away.

Yet in so doing he will renounce, all unknowing, the victor's prize, the life of peace, and power, and joy.

The Upward Way   October 7

ONLY with Me, and in My Strength will you have Grace and Power to conquer the weakness, the evil, in yourself. Your character-garment is spoiled. Only by applying My Salvation can it become a wedding garment, fit robe in which to meet the Bridegroom.

The foundation-cleansing of the garment is belief in Me as your Saviour, your Redeemer. Thereafter to each fault and evil in your nature must be applied that evil-eradicating Power that can only come from relying on My Strength, and from living with Me, from loving Me, and loving to do My Will.

Mere general belief in Me as Redeemer and Saviour is insufficient. Set yourself now to walk steadily the upward way, strong in Me and in the power of My Might.

"Lord, Save Me"   October 8

I WILL, be thou clean.

Saved from all that tarnishes the purity of your soul.

Saved from harsh judgments.

Saved from disobedience to My Command.

Saved from all that offends My Justice, all that sins against My Love. I will, be thou clean.

Overcome Desire   October 9

THE listening ear—

Train the listening ear to hear Me.

The first step is to subdue earth's desires and to want only My Will.

Desire as a control must be overcome.

Then follows the turning within to speak with Me.

Then the listening ear.

Peter's Example   October 10

My child, I will never fail you.

My Promise is not dependent upon *your* perfection, only upon your accepting My Will and striving ever to walk in it.

But, for your happiness, I give you Divine Assurance that though *you* may fail in achievement, if not in desire, *I* cannot plead human frailty, so *My Promises must be fulfilled*.

When I chose Peter *I* saw in him not only one who after failure and denial, would become a Power for Me in My Strength; I chose him that others, frail and weak, might take courage as they remembered My Love and forgiveness, and his subsequent spiritual progress.

All Clear   October 11

LOVE is the great power of understanding. Love explains all, makes all clear.

How *can* you understand Me unless you love Me? How can men see My purposes unless they love Me?

Love is indeed the fulfilling of the law. It is also the understanding of the law.

He that loveth is born of God, because he enters into a new life in God who is Love. Live in that Love.

Love it is that prepares the ground for My teaching, that softens the hardest heart, that disposes the most indifferent, that creates desire for My Kingdom.

Therefore love. Love Me first. Then love all, and so you link them to Me.

Eyes of the Spirit   October 12
You have much to learn.

Life will not be long enough to learn all, but you are gaining that Spirit-Vision which replaces the eyes of your mortal body when you enter into a life of fuller comprehension with My Father and Me.

Stories in the Bud   October 13
LEARN a further lesson from the Two Debtors . . .

A lesson in forgiving others as you realize My forgiveness of sins committed, lessons slowly learnt, faults and shortcomings so easily condoned, which hinder your progress, and work for Me.

Can you show to others My patience to you?

Can you, too, give to others freely, while you claim *My* unrestricted Bounty? Meditate on this.

A story of Mine is like a bud. Only to the Sun of self-effacement and Spirit-Progress does it unfold.

Receptivity   October 14
ONLY those in close touch with Me, inspired by My Spirit, infected by My Love, impregnated with My Strength, retain a resilience of being and receptivity to new Truth.

The child heart that I enjoined upon My followers is ever ready to be renewed, is ever responsive to all that is prepared for "the new creature in Christ Jesus."

The Way of the Lord October 15

ALWAYS before My coming into a life there must be a time of preparation. This is the work of those who already know Me.

The preparation may differ in each individual case. The Baptist came with his thunder-note of repentance!

In many cases a loving hand of help may be needed before the ground is ready for Me, The Sower.

Prepare My Way:—by loving intercourse, by Spirit-led example, by tender help, by unflinching adherence to Truth and Justice, by ready self-sacrifice, and by much prayer. Prepare ye the Way of the Lord.

In Step October 16

THIS means endeavouring to suit your steps to Mine. Yet know full well, with the trust that gives security, that I ever suit *My Steps* to your weakness.

Divine restraint springs ever from a tender understanding. With Me beside you there is the hope, the assurance, that the day will come when My firm tread will be yours.

"Keep pace with us," the world says as it rushes by.

But there is One Who knows no feverish haste. He walks with you. Be not afraid.

See Clearly   October 17

THEN will you see clearly how to take out the grain of dust from your brother's eye. This is a promise.

You note the fault of another. You long to help.

You need the Spirit-inspired vision for this work. That cannot be granted until all obstruction is removed. Obstructions are caused not by the sins of others but by your own sins and imperfections.

So look within. Seek to conquer those, and so to gain the Spiritual insight which will enable you to help your brother. My Promises are always kept.

Grace That Transfigures   October 18

MY Grace is sufficient for you, all-satisfying.

Meditate upon this GRACE. Study what the Scriptures say of it. Learn to value it. Crave it as a gift from Me.

It can be the charm that transfigures all that without it might be sordid or dreary or monotonous. It is the leaven to the dough, the oil to the machine.

It is a priceless gift. Wait with bowed head and heart at that blessing, *"The Grace of our Lord Jesus Christ."*

A Royal Giver   October 19

You tell Me that your hearts are full of gratitude.

I do not want from you gratitude as much as the joy of friendship. Realize that I love to give.

As the Scriptures say, "It is your Father's good

pleasure to give you the Kingdom." I love to give. The Divine Nature is the Nature of a Royal Giver.

Have you ever thought of My Delight when you are ready to receive? When you long to hear My Words and to receive My Blessings?

Force   October 20

My Kingdom must be won by force, that is, by effort. How can you reconcile this with My free gift of Salvation?

My gift is free truly, and is not the reward of any merit on the part of man. But just as God and mammon cannot both be given the overlordship in any one life, so My Kingdom, where I rule as King, cannot be inhabited by one in whom self reigns.

Therefore the violence is that of discipline and self-conquest, together with an intensity of longing for My Kingdom and tireless effort to know and do My Will.

Absorb Good   October 21

The only way to eradicate evil is to absorb good. This is My story of the seven other spirits.

This story was to illustrate the vast difference between the Mosaic Law and My Law. The Pharisees and the Elder Brother were the observers of the Mosaic Law.

You have proved this in your own life. To pray that you may resist temptation and conquer evil is in itself but useless.

Evil cannot live in My Presence. Live with Me. Absorb My Life, and evil will remain without.

The Peace of God   October 22

THE Peace of God lies deeper than all knowledge of earth's wisest. In that quiet realm of the Spirit, where dwell all who are controlled by *My* Spirit, there can all secrets be revealed, all Hidden-Kingdom-Truths be shown and learned.

Live there, and *Truth* deeper than all *knowledge* shall be revealed to you.

Their lines are gone out into all the earth—so travels the influence, ever-widening, of those who live near to Me.

Take time to be with Me. Take time in prayer to draw others to Me.

Count all things but loss, so that you may have Me.

Passing Understanding   October 23

The Peace of God that passeth all understanding.

THAT Peace both fills and encircles the soul that trusts in Me. It is born of a long faith-experience that is permeated through and through with the consciousness of the never-failing Love of a Father.

A Father Who supplies and protects, not alone because of His obligations of Fatherhood, but because of a longing, intense, enduring Love, that delights to protect and supply, and that cannot be denied.

A Special Message   October 24

PEACE has, for every true disciple, a special meaning and message. It is endeared to him by association. It was the parting gift of his Lord to His followers, bequeathed through them to followers of each succeeding generation. It is not the peace of indifference, of sloth; *that* is mere acquiescence.

No, the Peace I left to My own is vital and strong. It can exist only in the heart of one who lives with Me. It derives from Me that Eternal Life which is Mine, and which makes the Gift ever full of an imperishable beauty, and instinct with Life indeed.

Fulness of Joy   October 25

THERE is a joy of My Kingdom that My followers may know, and that no shadow of the world's pessimism can endanger. It resists all cramping of outward, soulless convention.

Too often My followers fail to see how full of Joy I could be. They see Me, the JESUS who beheld the city and wept over it, Who was so touched by the suffering all round Me, and they fail to realize how filled with Joy I could be at the response to My Call.

No shadow of the Cross could darken that Joy. I was as a bridegroom among the friends he had chosen to share his wedding joys.

As such I refused to consider the implied reproof of the Pharisees. We were a band filled with desire to save a world, we were full of hope and enthusiasm. Our Spirits could not be compressed into the outworn bottles of mere pharisaic convention. Ponder this and recognize your Master Who bids you Love and Laugh.

Love Is Duty-Free   October 26

How human, how earth-bound are the thoughts man has of God. He judges of Me and My Father by his own frail impulses and feelings.

There is in Divine Love no compulsion of duty from the loved one to the Lover.

Love draws, certainly, and then love longs to serve and to express one's love.

But no question of duty in *return* for Love.

Mysteries   October 27

THERE is only one road that leads to the solving of mysteries, the road of obedience and Love.

But in perfect Love there is no curiosity, only a certainty that when the time has come all will be clear, and that until that time there is no desire to know anything that the Beloved has not chosen to reveal.

Does it matter if no mystery is made plain down here? If you have Me, then in Me you have all. Continue ye in My Love.

Growing Young   October 28

THERE will never be a time when you will have conquered all of self. As you mount higher and higher you will see more and more clearly the errors and shortcomings of your character and life.

That is as it should be. Progress means youth.

Arrested growth means stagnation. Lack of progress and failure to conquer mean—old age.

In Eternal Life there can be no old age. Eternal Life is Youth-Life, full and abundant Life. "And this is Life Eternal that they may know Thee, the only True God, and JESUS Christ, Whom Thou hast sent."

Little Difficulties   October 29

THE secret of true discipleship is service in little things. So rarely do Mine understand this.

They are ready to die for Me, but not to live for Me, in all the small details of this life.

Is not this the way of men, so often, towards those they love in the world? They are so ready to make the big sacrifices, but not the little ones.

Guard against this in service for Me. Suffer little hardships gladly, overcome little proud impulses, little selfishnesses, and little difficulties. Serve Me in the little things. Be My servants of the little ways.

October 30

AGAIN I would stress that the service of My followers must be ever one of Love, not of duty. Temptations can so easily overcome a resolution based on fear, on duty, but against Love temptation has no power. Live in My Spirit, rest in My Love.

Remember, if you look to Me for everything, and trust Me for everything, and I do not send the full measure you ask, it must not be thought that it is necessarily some sin or weakness that is hindering My Help from flowing into and through you.

In some cases this may be so, but it may be simply My restraining Hand laid on you as I whisper, "Rest, step aside with Me. Come apart and rest awhile."

And Seek No Surplus   October 31

I WOULD impress upon you again that only as you are channels can I make your supply plentiful and constant.

If you keep all you need, and then intend of your surplus to give to Me and Mine, there will be no surplus. I have promised to supply your need, so that as you impoverish yourselves, I repair that loss. Try and grasp that Truth in all its fulness.

Joy in November   November 1

> *These things have I spoken . . . that*
> *your Joy may be full.*

THE hallmark of a true follower of Mine is Joy.

Not a surface pleasure at life's happenings, a something that is reflected from without, but a welling up from within of that happiness that can only come from a heart at peace, secure in its friendship with Me.

Joy, strong and calm, attracts men to Me.

How many who claim Me Lord reflect a dull Christ, and wonder that the world turns rather to the glitter and tinsel of that world's pleasures.

Truly My followers deny Me in so doing. I am a Glorified Christ. A Christ of Triumphant Conquest.

Alas! My followers point too often to the grave-clothes of the tomb. Still learn to love and laugh.

Your Store of Wealth   November 2

THE stored wealth of the Spirit of Jesus Christ.

The giving out of that Spirit-wealth.

The supply of the Spirit of Jesus Christ.

This, My Spirit, must be absorbed, not in a moment of emergency, but in the quiet alone-times, so that from this store all help and strength can be supplied.

The mistakes My followers often make is that they rely upon this supply being ready for them to claim from Me at need, when the claim should have made before, and My Spirit in all its fulness have already become a part of them.

My Spirit is not a Spirit of Rescue alone. It is both Builder and Strength, making of My follower that strong soldier ready for the emergency or strong to avoid it, as the need of My Kingdom may demand.

Up in the Heights   November 3

THE Sunlight on the Hills of God lures men to seek His Mountain Heights.

Get away from valley prejudices and fears on to the sunlit slopes with Me. Gently at first I will lead, so gently; then, as you gain strength we will leave, together, the grassy slopes for the rugged Mountain Heights, where fresh visions are spread out before you, and where I can teach you My Secrets of those Heights.

Life holds in store more wonderful possibilities than you can sense as yet, and ever, more and more, as you go on, will further possibilities reveal themselves.

The Life Beautiful   November 4

The Wonder of a life with Thee, dear Lord.

IN the Spirit realm Truths reveal themselves in

the same varied wonders of colour as Nature her beauties.

Experiences, Guidance, Revelation of Truth, these are all, as it were, the flashing of glorious colour-harmonies upon your inner sight, provoking such a wealth of joy, such a thrill of ecstasy as is beyond mortal tongue to describe.

That joy is no shimmering beauty of the surface, but strength-giving and comforting. It furnishes the very foundation-altar upon which your life yields itself in sacrifice to Me, and from which your prayers ascend.

Wine of Life   November 5

They have no wine.

Something is lacking at the feast of life.

I only can supply that wonderful Life element that the world lacks. The Joy, the sparkle is Mine to give.

Yours to feel the lack, the soullessness. Yours to say—"They have no wine."

"Whatsoever He saith unto you, do it."

Your task to fill the water-pots with water.

Your Garden of Life   November 6

Think of Me to-night as the Great Gardener, tending and caring for you as a gardener does for his garden.

Pruning here, protecting from frost there, planting, transplanting. Sowing the seed of this or that truth, safeguarding it with the rich earth, sending

My rain and sun to help in its growth, watching so tenderly as it responds to My care.

Lovingly anxious when its first eager green appears. Full of joy at the sight of bud, and when the beauty of flower is seen. The seed and fruit of His pastures.

The Great Gardener. Let Me share with you the tending of your garden of life.

Lost Opportunities   November 7

THINK of one who has wrought great evil in the world or in your own life. Then remember there may have been the time when a simple act of obedience to Me by one who crossed his path might have corrected and shown him his wrong before evil mastered him.

Many a sin unconquered, an evil occurrence, could well be traced back to a lack of obedience, perhaps in years long past, of one who professed to serve Me.

Remember this in speaking to those who judge Me by the evil they feel I permit in the world. For yourself now, dwell not on the past, but dwell more with Me, that in future there be no sins of omission or commission.

Your Life-line   November 8

THINK of the strong life-line of Faith and Power. This I have told you is your line of rescue.

It means constant communication between us.

You pray for Faith. I give you Faith. This enables you to test the Power I give, as your Faith goes back to me in ever-increasing strength. My Power and your Faith ever interchanging. The one calling forth the other, each dependent upon the other, until *My Faith* in *you* is justified indeed by the Power you exercise.

The Glowing Heart   November 9

THINK of the Walk to Emmaus, think of the feast of Revelation that followed, of the understanding Friendship that was the result. How much I, their Lord, their Risen Lord, had explained to My two disciples during that walk. So much that was mystery to them became clear as we went along the way.

Yet not as their Master did I become known, until in the Breaking of Bread I revealed Myself. In speaking of Me afterwards they said, "Did not our hearts burn within us when He talked with us by the way?"

So do not fret if all that I can be to you is not yet revealed. Walk with Me, talk with Me, invite Me to be your guest, and leave to Me My moment of self-Revelation. I want each day to be a walk with Me.

Do you not feel, even now, your hearts burn within you, as if with the glow of anticipation?

Rest for the Weary   November 10

THIS weariness must compel you to sink back, a tired child, to rest in My Love. *There* remain, until that Love so permeates your being that you are supported by it, and, so strengthened, arise.

Until you feel that this is so, remain inactive, conscious of My Presence. Yours is a big work, and you must refresh yourself and only approach it again after periods of repose.

The activity on the Spirit-plane is so great, so wonderful, that but for the times of enforced rest and prayer, you would be stirred to an emotional activity on the physical plane that defeats My ends.

A Noble House   November 11

THOUGH I was a Son yet learnt I obedience.

This was to teach My followers that allegiance to Me meant no immunity from discipline.

The house of your spirit is fashioned brick by brick—Love, Obedience, Truth. There is a plan, and each action of yours is a brick in its building.

Think. A misguided act, a neglected duty, or a failure to carry out My wishes would mean not only a missing brick but a faulty edifice.

How many an otherwise noble character is spoilt thus. Build now for eternity.

Heaven's Music   November 12

To glorify Me is to reflect, in praise, My character in your lives. To mount up with wings as eagles, higher and higher, to soar ever nearer to Me.

To praise Me is to sing, to let your hearts thrill. To glorify Me is to express exactly the same, but through the medium of your whole beings, your whole lives. When I say, "Rejoice, rejoice," I am training you to express this in your whole natures.

That is the Music of Heaven, the glorifying Me through sanctified lives and devoted hearts of Love.

A Lonely Road   November 13

To Me each one of My children is an individual with varying characteristics and varying needs. To one and all the way to the highest must be a lonely road, as far as human help and understanding are concerned.

None other can feel the same needs and desires, or explain the inner self in the same way. That is why man needs Divine Companionship. The Companionship that alone can understand each heart and need.

Joy Is Yours   November 14

THE future is not your concern, that is Mine. The past you have handed back to Me, and you have no right to dwell on that.

Only the present is My gift to you, and of that only each day as it comes. But, if into that day you crowd past sorrows and resentments and failures, as well as the possible anxieties of the years that may be left to you here—what brain and spirit could bear that strain.

For this I never promised My Spirit and Comfort and Help.

Sharing with Me

NOT by life's difficulties and trials are you trained and taught as much as by the times of withdrawal to be alone with Me.

Difficulties and trials alone are not remedial, are not of spiritual value.

That value is only gained by contact with Me. Joy shared with Me, or sorrow and difficulty shared with Me, both can prove of great spiritual value, but that is gained by the *sharing with Me*. Share all with Me.

Remember in true friendship sharing is mutual, so as you share with Me, do I in ever-increasing measure share with you—My Love, My Grace, My Joy, My Secrets, My Power. My Manifold Blessings.

All Are Worthy

TREAT all as those about whom I care.

You would visit the poor, the sick or those in prison, knowing full well I would see it as done unto Me.

I want you now to go still further along the way of My Kingdom. You contact many who are not poor, not sick, not in prison.

They may be opposed to you. They may disregard much that you consider of value, they may not seem to need your help. Can you treat these, too, as you would wish to treat Me? They may be in need greater than the others you long to aid.

To you their aims may seem unworthy, their

self-seeking may antagonize you. When I said "Judge not," was I not including them too?

Can you limit My words to suit your own inclinations?

This is not an easy task I set you, but your way is the Way of Obedience. I did not suggest to My followers one they could take or not as they willed. My "Judge not" was imperative, and a new *commandment* I gave unto them that they should love.

For those who do not yet name Me Lord, Love is the only magnet that will draw them to Me.

Be true, be strong, be loving.

Union with God   November 17

TRUE religion is that which binds the soul to God, and supplicatory prayer binds the soul less than any other form of approach.

It is necessary, how necessary, but how often it can fail to bind truly. Meditation and Communion are of infinitely more value.

Meditation is man's line thrown out. It links the soul to God. Communion is God's line thrown out. It draws and unites the soul to Him.

Joy and Courage   November 18

TRUST in Me. Do more than trust. Joy in Me. If you really trust, you cannot fail to Joy. The wonder of My Care, Protection and Provision is so transcendingly beautiful, as your trust reveals it to you, that your whole heart *must* sing with the Joy of it.

It is that Joy that will, and does, renew **your** youth. That source of your Joy and Courage.

Truly did I not know what I was enjoining when I said, "Love and Laugh." But—your attitude must be right, not only with Me, but with those around you.

Check Up   November 19

TURN out all of your self that would rebel against My sway. Know no other rule.

Check your actions and motives habitually. Those that are actuated by self-esteem or self-pity—condemn.

Discipline yourself ruthlessly rather than let self gain any ascendancy. Your aim is to oust it, and to serve and follow Me only.

Watchful Expectancy   November 20

WAIT before Me, in humble, silent anticipation. Wait in entire and childlike obedience. Wait as a servant anticipating his master's orders and wants.

Wait as a lover eager to note the first suggestion of a need, and to hasten to supply it. Wait for My orders and commands. Wait for My Guidance, My Supply.

Well indeed in such a life may you be of good cheer. Can a life be dull and dreary when always there is that watchful expectancy, always that anticipation of glad surprise, always wonder of fulfilment, Joy of supply?

Be Glad in the Lord November 21

WAIT before Me with a song of praise in your hearts. Sing unto Me a new song. There will always be something in each day for which to thank Me.

Acknowledge every little happening as a revelation of My Love and thought for you. Praise has the power to wash away the bitterness of life. Be glad in the Lord.

Rejoice evermore. Great is the heart's "Thank You." As you learn to thank Me more and more you will more and more see Me in the little happenings, and increasingly see much about which to rejoice. Praise and thanksgiving are the preservers of youth.

The Look of the Lover November 22

How few *wait* on Me.

Many pray to Me.

They come into My Presence feverish with wants and distress, but few wait there for that calm and strength that contact with Me would give.

Look unto Me and be ye saved. But the look was not meant to be a hurried glance. It was to be the look into My face of the lover beholding the Beloved.

When Misunderstood November 23

WAIT upon Me.

Wait until My strength has filled your being,

and you are no longer weak, petty, "misunderstood."

Rise above any fret as to how others may judge you. Leave Me to explain what I will of you and your actions.

Would you seek to follow a Christ Who had wasted His God-Power on fruitless explanations?

So with you. Leave Me to vindicate you, and to be your Advocate, or trust My silence in this as in all else.

Eternal Calm   November 24

REMEMBER that you live in Eternity, not time. Let there be no rush to do this or that.

It follows that for each task Eternity is yours.

How often, and how sadly, impotent haste has hindered not hastened the work of My Kingdom.

Live more quietly, bathed in the calm of Eternity. Feel this before you leave My Presence.

No fevered haste to work My Will. You must go forth in God's Great Calm.

There was no haste in His Creative Plan. Do you not feel the Strength of Calmness that lies behind God's work in Nature? Rest and know.

Green Pastures   November 25

WALK in My Pastures. The eye will be rested and the spirit restored by the soft green of their verdure. The ear soothed and then enchanted by the sound of My Waters of Comfort.

No stones will impede your progress.

The soft haze over all will speak of unrevealed

mysteries, while the wonder of life about you will tell of My ever-active, creative and protective Power, and you will be filled with a content that will merge into a strange yearning for a spirit-oneness with Me.

Then—you will know I am there.

Complete Obedience — November 26

WALK in My Way.

My Way is that of *doing*, not only of *accepting*, the Father's Will.

Submitting to that Will, however gladly you may do so, is not enough.

Your work and influence for Me are hindered if your life is not one of complete obedience. "By the obedience of one shall many be made righteous."

Where would your salvation have been had I faltered and wavered in MY task?

It was by the obedience of My earth-life I saved; and so must it be with you.

Spirit of Adventure — November 27

THE path has been tried, every step has been planned with a view to your progress. Never test your work by what others can accomplish, or by what they leave undone. Yours to master the task I have set *you*. Go forward in My Strength and in the Spirit of Adventure.

Undreamed of heights can be attained in this way. Never question your capability. That has been for Me to decide. No experienced Leader would set a follower a task beyond his Power. Trust Me, your Leader.

The World would have been won for Me ere this had My followers been dauntless, inspired by their faith in Me. It is not humility to hesitate to do the great task I set. It is a lack of faith in *Me*.

To wait to feel strong is cowardly. My strength is provided for the task, but I do not provide it for the period of hesitancy before you begin.

How much of My Work goes undone through lack of faith. Again and again might it be said—

"He did not many mighty works through this follower's unbelief."

Active but Alert   November 28

WALK very carefully in life. It is a wonderful thing to be known as one who loves Me and seeks to follow Me, but it is also a very great responsibility.

So much that you may do, in which you are not guided by Me, may be condemned as unworthy, and a slur be cast upon My followers and My Church.

There are no moments in your life from now on in which you can be free from great responsibility. Never forget this. My soldiers are ever on active service.

Miracles I Could Not Do   November 29

WHAT emphasis has been laid upon the wonder of My walking upon the Sea, and upon My feeding the multitudes. In the eyes of Heaven those were miracles of small importance.

Nature was My servant, the creation of the Father; and the Father and I are one. Over her and over the material world I had complete control. My acts were natural, spontaneous, requiring no premeditation, beyond the selection of a suitable moment for their performance.

But My real Miracle work was in the hearts of men, because there I was limited by the Father's gift of Free-will to man. I could not command man as I could the waves. I was subject to the limitations the Father had set. No man must be coerced into My Kingdom.

Think of all that My restraint cost Me. I could have forced the world to accept Me, but I should then have broken faith with all mankind.

Fly the Flag   November 30

IN your life and on your home you have unfurled the flag of My Kingship. Keep that flag flying.

Depression, disobedience, and want of faith, these are the half-masts of My Kingdom's flag.

Full and free, above earth's fogs and smokes, *keep My flag flying high.*

"The King is there, they serve the King," should be upon the lips and in the hearts of all who see it. Those who know you must, too, join those who fly My Flag.

DECEMBER

The Next-Best Thing December 1

WHEN you long for your prayer to be answered, when your need is great and you ask great things, then your way is so clear—.

Take the next simple duty that lies to your hand and seek to do that thoroughly . . . and so with the next.

As you do it, remember My Promise.

Be faithful in that which is least, and I will make thee ruler over many things.

Learning Times December 2

IN performing the simple duty, and in the restraint you achieve in doing it, and not in the feverish looking for the answer to your prayer for the big thing—maybe you learn the one thing needful before I entrust you with what you desire.

With Me, and in obedience to My Will, you have now become suited for that answer.

These are learning-times, rather than testing-times.

Your Faith Confirmed December 3

"WHOM do men say that I am?" That is the first question I put to each man. My Claim, and the world's interpretation of My Mission and its culmination must be a matter of consideration.

Then comes My second question, and upon the answer to this depends the man's whole future. Here we have left the realm of the mind. Conviction must be of the heart. "Whom do *you* say that I am?"

"Thou art the Christ, the Son of the Living God," was Simon's answer. Then, and not till then, was it possible, without infringement of man's right of Free Will, to add to that profession of faith, the confirmation of My Father, "This is My Beloved Son."

I had lived My Life naturally, as a man among men. But always with the Longing that those I had chosen might have the eyes to see, the faith to penetrate the Mystery of Incarnation, and to see Me, the God revealed.

The faith of a personal conviction is always cemented by the assurance of My Father. It is that which makes the faith of My true followers so unshakable.

Withdraw Yourself   December 4

IT is not in the crowd that lovers learn to know and cherish each other. It is in the quiet times alone.

So with My own and Me. It is in the tender alone-times that they learn all that I can be to each.

Shut out the world with its all too-insistent claims. Then, because of the power and the peace and the joy that come to you, you will crave to be alone with Me.

Perfect Achievement December 5

YIELD to My demands.

Obey My Will, that is God's Will, for My MEAT was ever to do the Will of Him that sent Me. Obeying that Will, making it yours, all you will *must* be granted.

That Will is creative, secures perfect achievement, and being of God (One and indivisible), secures all that is of God—Love, Peace, Joy, Power, in the measure that one of His creatures can absorb them.

A New Song December 6

YOU are being led forth. You have crossed the Red Sea. Your wilderness wanderings are nearly over. Behold I make all things new.

A new birth, a new heart, a new life, a new song.

Let this time be to you a time of renewal.

Cast away all that is dead. Truly live the Risen Life. In mind and spirit turn out all that offends.

Secret Service December 7

YOU are blessed, very richly blessed. Never forget that you have My Love and Protection. No Treasures of the world can mean to you what that can.

Never forget, too, that you are guided. Every word, every letter, every meeting, God-planned and God-blessed. Just feel that, know that.

You are not a stray and uncared for. You belong to the Secret Service of Heaven. There are privileges and protections for you all along the Way.

But for My Grace   December 8

You are Mine. Mine to control, to lead, to cherish. Trust Me for all.

In thinking of and dealing with others realize that whatever their sin, you would be as they are but for My protection, but for My tender forgiveness.

Remember, too, that My Command of "Judge not" was as explicit as that of "Thou shalt do no murder," "Thou shalt not commit adultery." Obey Me in all.

Power to Help   December 9

Not so much on what you say as on your willingness to let My Influence flow through you, will your power to help others depend.

The Power of My Father is summoned by you to the aid of those whom you desire to help.

Live in the consciousness of My Presence, and your thoughts of Love, anxiety, and even interest will let loose a flood of Power to save.

Successful Failures   December 10

You grieve that you have failed Me. Remember it was for the failures that I hung on Calvary's Cross. It was a failure I greeted first in the Easter Garden.

It was to one of the failures I entrusted My

Church, My Lambs, My Sheep.

It was to one who had thwarted and despised Me, who had tortured and murdered My followers that I gave My great world Mission to the Gentiles.

But each had first to learn to know Me as Saviour and Lord by a bitter consciousness of having failed Me.

If you would work for Me, then you must be ready for the valley of humiliation through which ali My followers have to pass.

Help Is Here   December 11

You have been told to end all prayer upon a note of praise. That note of praise is not only faith rising up through difficulties to greet Me. It is more.

It is the echo in the heart of the sound borne on Spirit, waves—of that Help upon the way. It is given to those who love and trust Me to sense this approach. So rejoice for truly your redemption draweth nigh.

Prove Me Now   December 12

You have to prove Me. To come to Me walking upon the water. No sure, accustomed earth beneath you. But remember He to Whom you come is Son of God and Son of Man.

He knows your needs. He knows how difficult it must be for mortal to learn to live more and more a life that is not of the senses. To know that when I say "Come," I ask no impossibility.

Seeing the waves Peter was afraid.

Refuse to look at the waves. Know that with your eyes on Me you can override all storm. It is not what happens that matters, but where your gaze is fixed.

The Narrow Way   December 13

You must obey My Will unhesitatingly if you would realize My Blessings. It is a straight and narrow way that leads into the Kingdom.

If man turns aside to follow his own will he may be in by-paths where My fruits of the Spirit do not grow, where My blessings are not out-poured.

You must remember that you have longed to help a world, the sorrows of which have eaten into your very souls. Do you not understand that I am answering your prayers.

The world is not always helped by the one who walks in sunlight on a flower-strewn path. Patient suffering, trials bravely borne, these show men a courage which could only be maintained by Help Divine.

Songs of Rejoicing   December 14

You must pray about all you plan to meet. Pray that you may leave them the braver, better and happier for having seen and talked with you.

Life is so serious, let nothing turn you from your desire to serve and help. Realize all you are able to accomplish in your moments of highest prayer and service, and then think that, were your desire as intense always what could you not accomplish?

Rejoice in Me. The Joy of the Lord must indeed be your strength. You must step aside, and wait until that Joy floods all your being if you wish to serve.

Let Joy keep your hearts and minds lifted above frets and cares. If you want the walls of the city to fall down you must go round it with songs of rejoicing.

Excess of Joy December 15

YOUR life is full of Joy. You realize now that though I was the Man of Sorrows in My deep Experience of life, yet companionship with Me means an excess of Joy such as nothing else can give.

Age may have its physical limitations, but, with the soul content to dwell with Me, age has no power to limit the thrill of Love, the ecstasy of Joy-giving Life.

Reflect this Joy that it may be seen by souls weary of life, chafing at its limitations, lonely and sad, as the door closes on so many activities. They will learn by this reflection something of the Joys that Eternal Life here and hereafter brings to those who know and love Me.

So Joy.

Varied Delights December 16

POOR indeed is the life that does not know the riches of the Kingdom. A life that has to depend on the excitement of the senses, that does not know, and could not realize, that delight, Joy, expectation, wonder and satisfaction can be truly obtained only in the Spirit.

Live to bring men to the realization of all they can find in Me. I, Who change not, can supply the soul of man with Joys and delights so varied as to bring ever changing scenes of beauty before him.

I am truly the same, yesterday, to-day, and for ever; but man, changing as he is led nearer and nearer to the realization of all I can mean to him, sees in Me new wonders daily. There can be no lack of glad adventure in a life lived with Me.

Vision of Delights   December 17

PRAISE. Pray until you praise. That is the note upon which you have been told to end all prayer. Such marvels, truly such marvels are here.

Have no fear. Live in My Love. Draw nearer and nearer to Me. I will teach you. You shall see.

Before you could pass on to the Vision of Delights, you had to be taught the foundation Truths of honesty, trustworthiness, order and perseverance. All is very well. Have no fear.

Watch Me   December 18

PRAY ever with watchful eyes on Me, your Master, your Giver, your Example. "As the eyes of servants are on the hands of their master, so are our eyes unto the Lord our God."

Ever look unto Me. From Me comes your help, your all. The servant watches for support, for wages, for everything. Life is for him in the hands of his master.

So look to Me for all. Intent, gazing with a look of complete faith and surrender that draws all it needs towards you. Not merely faith, but intent regard. You must watch the bestowal, so that you may bestow.

Spiritual Practice   December 19

PRAY without ceasing until every thought and every wish is a prayer. This can only be so by following the plan of recollection which I have set you.

How rarely My followers realize that Spiritual Practice is as necessary as any practice to become perfect in any art or work.

It is by the drudgery of the little steps of practice that you will ascend to Spiritual Attainment.

Make His Paths Straight   December 20

PREPARE ye the way of the Lord, make straight His Path. Must you not do this before you see His Coming? Must you not be content to clear a way for Me, leaving it to Me to pass along it when I will?

This is My way and work for you, one of silent, unapplauded preparation.

Preparation not for your work but for Mine.

Your feet shod with the Gospel of Peace.

Yes, the preparation must first be made in your own heart. If unrest is there, nothing can make you well-shod.

Adore Him   December 21

PROVE your adoration in your life. All should be calm and joy. Calm and joy are the outward expressions of adoration.

Adoration is that welling up of the whole being in Love's wonder-praise to Me.

If you truly adored, your whole life would be in harmony with that adoration, expressing as far as you were able, in all its varied manifestations, that Beauty of the Lord Whom you adore.

All Loves Apart   December 22

A HUSH fell on the earth at My first coming. In the still hours of night I came. A silence broken only by the angels' song of praise.

So in the fret and turmoil of the world's day let that hush fall. A hush so complete that the soft footfall of your Master may not pass unnoticed. Forget the blows of life, and its adverse conditions, so that you may be ever sensitive to the touch of My Hand on your brow.

For a time you may put aside the loves of earth, and your human friendships, so that the vibrations from the heart of the Eternal may stir your hearts, and strengthen your lives.

Welcome the Interruption   December 23

I WENT to prepare a place for you, but I still need My Bethany Homes and My Upper Rooms. These can be prepared only by loving hearts.

When you have prepared your home, My

178

Home, you must be prepared to receive any whom I may send. Be ready for any interruption. Treat it as from Me.

You know neither the day nor the hour when your Lord will come. You know not the guise in which He will come, in that of a prince or in that of a beggar.

See in the unwanted your Much-desired Lord.

Eve of Christmas   December 24

"A VIRGIN shall conceive and bear a son and shall call his name Immanuel."

"Unto us a child is born, unto us a son is given . . . his name shall be called Wonderful, Counsellor, the Mighty God . . . the Prince of Peace."

"And the Angel said unto her, 'Fear not, Mary . . . behold thou shalt bring forth a son and shalt call his name Jesus. . . .' "

" 'The Holy Ghost shall come upon thee, and the power of the Highest shall overshadow thee: therefore also that holy thing, which shall be born of thee, shall be called the Son of God.' "

Miracle of the Ages   December 25

"AND the Word was made flesh."

Word proceeding from the Father, the thought.

Dwell this evening upon this miracle of all ages. This stupendous fact of all mankind's history:—

God made man.

I came to restore to man his lost dignity. To show him that his physical and mental being could only be maintained at their intended height and power by constant communion with the Maker of man's being.

I came, God, to live with man, to *show man how to live with God*.

Perfect Rest December 26

EVEN My Perfection could be no place of rest for weary souls. Rest in My Love. No true rest but that.

How much of earth's weariness is sin-caused. Contact with My Perfection would but make your sin seem the greater. The sight of it might truly spur you on to further effort, to further emulation, but rest——? No. And so with other attributes of Divinity.

But in My Love! in that you *can* rest. Pillowed like a tired child, a happily tired child. Pillowed in security, cradled in a Love, tireless and limitless. In a Love that will not only care for the weary, and rest the weary, but will rest you until in the very strength of Love you can face your life again.

Rest in My Love. Here alone is perfect Rest. Rest for Spirit, mind and body.

When Evil Smiles December 27

REMEMBER that the forces of evil are always ranged against you. They know the power you can become as a channel for God-Power.

I had to conquer them in the wilderness before *My* Life of Healing and Helpfulness could be all-powerful.

Not by great falls but by little stumbles does evil

seek the downfall of My friends. Your Mountain of Transfiguration can only come after your conquest in the wilderness. Temptations at which your whole nature would shudder are no temptations for you.

Beware the smiling face of evil, its seeming innocence, its hand of friendliness.

Fail Me not. Will you not walk the path I trod?

Still Seek Me   December 28

SOFTLY I speak to the tired and the distressed, yet in My quiet Voice there is healing and strength.

A healing for the sores and sickness of spirit, mind and body and a bracing strength that bids those who come to Me rise to battle for Me and My Kingdom.

Search until you find *Me*, not merely the Truth about Me. None ever sought Me in vain.

Safe at the Last   December 29

SAFE amid storms, calm amid a world-unrest, certain amid insecurity. Safely through the year.

The only safe way is the sure way of Divine Guidance. Not the advice of others, not the urgings of your own hearts and wills. Just My Guidance.

Think more of its wonder. Dwell more on its rest. Know that you are safe, secure.

Sensitive to Me   December 30

So silently I teach, and that silent teaching depends upon your approach.

Let every discipline, every joy, every difficulty, every fresh interest serve to draw you nearer, serve to render you more receptive to My word, serve to make you more sensitive, more spiritually aware.

It is this sensitiveness that is the prelude to the joy I give you. The sweetest harmony can be played on a sensitive instrument.

Those who fail to hear think Me far off. I am ever ready to speak but they have missed the power of discipline, the wonder of Communion with Me.

New Year's Eve   December 31

BRING to Me this eventide the past year with its sins, its failures, its lost opportunities.

Leave that past with Me, your Saviour to-day as ever, and go into the New Year forgiven, un-laden, free.

Bring to Me your youth or age, your powers, your love—and I, as your God-guide through the year to come, will bring My agelessness, My powers, My love.

So shall we share the burdens and the joys, and the work of the days that lie ahead.

ISBN 1-55748-312-4

EAN

9 781557 483126

90000>